Make It So

Leadership Lessons from

Make It So

Leadership Lessons from

STAR TREK
THE NEXT GENERATION®

Wess Roberts, Ph.D.,

author, Leadership Secrets of
Attila the Hun

and

Bill Ross

POCKET BOOKS

New York   London   Toronto   Sydney   Tokyo   Singapore

POCKET BOOKS, a division of Simon & Schuster Inc.
1230 Avenue of the Americas, New York, NY 10020

A VIACOM COMPANY

STAR TREK is a Registered Trademark of
Paramount Pictures.

This book is published by Pocket Books, a division of
Simon & Schuster Inc., under exclusive license from
Paramount Pictures.

Library of Congress Catalog Card Number: 95-22323

ISBN: 0-671-52097-0

First Pocket Books hardcover printing September 1995

10 9 8 7 6 5 4 3 2 1

Printed in the U.S.A.

This book is for Justin, Jaime, and Jeremy
with every confidence that they will always
engage wisdom whenever and wherever
they lead in their generation.
And for Cheryl,
who has always led well.

It is also for Susan, Bill's Number One,
and the rest of the crew he calls family.

Contents

Author's Note

Late in his career, I had the occasion to meet Raymond Burr, who played the lead role in the *Perry Mason* television series. During our brief conversation, I happened to mention to him that Cheryl was a devout fan of his and both the original and new *Perry Mason* series. I then emphasized just how devotedly Cheryl followed the series by commenting that I believed she could perhaps recite most of his lines from the various *Perry Mason* episodes.

Being the gracious man that he was, Mr. Burr thanked me for mentioning this to him and asked me to tell Cheryl that he appreciated her enthusiasm for his work and the series. On reflection, what he said next should not have come as a surprise to me, but at the time it was a new and interesting perspective. He said that while Cheryl might find enjoyment memorizing his character's lines from past episodes, as an actor, it was far more important for him to concentrate on the lines he had to learn for future performances.

There is a valuable principle that can be learned from this brief conversation. While the past affords us the opportunity to learn many useful lessons that can be applied in the present, we can also gain insight for today by giving some thoughtful consideration as to what lies ahead for us in the future.

And so it is that while my earlier books presented leadership lessons that can be learned from a controversial leader who lived in a time long in our past, this work presents leadership lessons that can be learned from a fictional character who lives four hundred years in the future. Indeed, it is necessary that we be prepared to lead well in the present and that we acquire those leadership qualities that will become absolutely vital to our success as leaders in the future.

As I began work on this book, little did I realize just how rich STAR TREK: THE NEXT GENERATION is in illustrating the timeless leadership qualities that are as indispensable for those who lead today as they will be for those who lead tomorrow. I am now convinced that viewing the episodes from this series can also teach us valuable lessons about respect for life and acceptance of people without regard to race, gender, or culture. In viewing these episodes, one can also learn a great deal about the value of others' views and opinions, and that the unknown is not to be feared, but understood. Moreover, in our day of tumult and intolerance, it is altogether refreshing to view leaders possessing those qualities that give us hope for a better future.

For these reasons, I believe that STAR TREK: THE NEXT GENERATION provides a powerful metaphorical setting, and that Captain Jean-Luc Picard is a compelling protagonist, who exemplifies all of the leadership qualities illustrated and discussed in *Make It So*. Those readers who are familiar with the character, Captain Picard, already know him to be the leader that we all wish we worked for, whose leadership gives us confidence and comfort in meeting the challenges we face each and every day, and the type of leader that we should strive to become.

This book is written for both the Trekker and non-Trekker alike. To accommodate those readers unfamiliar with STAR TREK, a brief history of this series from *The Original Series* to *The Next Generation* is provided as an appendix to this book. Similarly, a cast of characters and a list of STAR TREK terms are also included as appendices.

Make It So is written as a collection of anecdotes and observations that come from selected experiences of Captain Picard and the crew of the *U.S.S. Enterprise* during their seven-plus years of voyages throughout the galaxy. These anecdotes are based on episodes from STAR TREK: THE NEXT GENERATION, but are retold through the eyes and in the words of Captain Picard. As such, he reveals his thoughts and emotions about these experiences and the leadership lessons they contain on a much more personal level than portrayed in the series. And even though these episodic experiences are taken from a science-fiction series set in the future, their underlying themes and messages are not so different from the real-life situations and circumstances each of us encounter daily.

The introduction for *Make It So* recounts the episode that I have chosen to give Captain Picard both a reason and motive for preparing leadership lessons based upon his experiences as the commanding officer of the Federation's flagship, the *U.S.S. Enterprise.*

Although a fictional character, STAR TREK's Captain Picard is not without flaw and has experienced many of the same kinds of problems and challenges you and I experience in our own lives. Moreover, developing the leadership qualities and poise that Jean-Luc has illustrated in *The Next Generation* is well within the reach of anyone who has the will and the courage to lead well. Some interesting aspects of Captain Picard's life leading up to the point in his career where he is given command of the *U.S.S. Enterprise*-D are included in the background section of this book.

Each chapter begins with a foreword that provides a general introduction to its theme. In keeping with the fictional authenticity of this book, whose primary audience is future cadets at Starfleet Academy, these are written by Admiral Andrea Brand, the Academy's superintendent. The foreword is followed by Captain Picard's summary of an episodic experience, which serves as the anecdotal illustration for the observations and lessons that follow. And while each of the nine leadership qualities discussed in this book is actually manifested by Captain Picard and/or other characters in the episode being recounted, these qualities were actually derived from several years of my research on leadership. But if you would like to think of them as qualities that Jean-Luc derived on his own, it will bother me not at all.

The leadership qualities in *Make It So* are presented in their rank order of importance rather than according to the chronological sequence of the STAR TREK: THE NEXT GENERATION episodes used to illustrate them. However, the fact is that these qualities are neither mutually exclusive nor manifest in isolation. If anything, these are interdependent qualities of effective, competent leadership.

Make It So concludes with an epilogue, which serves as Captain Picard's opportunity to remind us that the merits of one's leadership—fairly or unfairly—are always under scrutiny. It is a leader's responsibility to proceed with his duties without regard to being under constant examination. Indeed, the best of leaders needn't be reminded or compelled by others to do what is right.

Wess Roberts
Sandy, Utah
March 1995

Introduction

"Legacy"

Superintendent's note. *A man's learning, experiences, and wisdom need not die with him, but may live forever if recorded as his legacy.*
Admiral Andrea Brand
Superintendent, Starfleet Academy

Captain's personal journal: Stardate 41419.1. Departing Relva VII.

I find myself greatly surprised to have just been subjected to the most intensive investigation of my character and fitness to command that I have ever experienced in my thirty-nine-year career as an officer in Starfleet. Although a starship is subject to routine command inspections, this grueling scrutiny was quite unexpected. Perhaps even more disturbing to me was

1

learning that this investigation was initiated at the insistence of an old friend, Admiral Gregory Quinn. I now understand that his motivation for this surprise inspection was based on concern for Federation security . . . the admiral and a few others at Starfleet Command suspect a conspiracy against the Federation. The fact remains that these suspicions fall short of justifying the evasive fashion by which Admiral Quinn directed his unannounced investigation of the *Enterprise* and me. Quite simply, the whole affair was a charade, from start to finish, and it placed a great strain on both the *Enterprise*'s staff and my longtime friendship with Admiral Quinn.

In parking orbit at Relva VII, we were transporting Wesley Crusher to Starfleet facilities where he was to sit for competitive testing against other finalists for admission to Starfleet Academy. To my great surprise, I learned that Admiral Quinn was on Relva VII and had requested to be beamed aboard the *Enterprise* immediately. Once on board, Admiral Quinn and Lieutenant Commander Dexter Remmick, an officer the admiral brought aboard with him, met with me privately. During our brief meeting, Admiral Quinn informed me that Commander Remmick was with the Inspector General's Office and would be conducting a full investigation of the *Enterprise*. When I asked my longtime friend why this investigation was necessary, he simply but bluntly told me that he had reason to believe something was wrong with my ship. I was ordered to give Commander Remmick my full cooperation and directed to inform my staff that they were to do likewise. Frankly, it was difficult for any of us to sense a single problem aboard the *Enterprise* worthy of Admiral Quinn's concern. I also assure you that it was quite difficult to restrain ourselves when confronted by Commander Remmick's intrusive and harassing questions.

At the conclusion of his investigation, Commander Remmick reported to Admiral Quinn that he couldn't find what my old friend had asked for, either through lengthy interviews with my officers or upon detailed examination of the ship's logs. Although thorough in his efforts, Mr. Remmick said he could find no problems at all . . . except perhaps . . . a casual familiarity among the bridge crew, as if finding at least one *problem* would please the admiral. But he quickly surmised this intimacy *problem* to come mostly from our sense of teamwork and feeling of family. Commander Remmick's observation seemed to be his way of canceling out casual familiarity as a *problem* of concern.

As Mr. Remmick departed my conference room, he paused at the door and remarked that his tour of duty with the Inspector General's Office would be over in six months and upon completion of his present assignment he wished to be assigned to the *Enterprise*. In making this request, Commander Remmick simultaneously put his stamp of approval on my fitness to command and our casual familiarity on the bridge.

His investigation over and with only the two of us

present, Admiral Quinn told me not to judge his or Commander Remmick's actions too harshly. It seems that he and others at Starfleet Command had to be very sure of me. They had become suspicious of certain problems in the Federation. They believed someone or something to be attempting to destroy the very fabric of everything the Federation had been trying to build up in the last two hundred years. He would say no more as to what evidence they had. Too many people were involved. Furthermore, he still didn't know if the threat came from inside or outside the Federation. My old friend said he needed people he could trust in strong positions throughout the Federation. My pledge of personal support was not enough. He wanted to promote me to the rank of admiral and appoint me as commandant of Starfleet Academy.

I was dismayed to learn that there had never been a problem with the *Enterprise*. The entire point of Admiral Quinn's investigation was to make sure that I had not sided with whomever or whatever was threatening the Federation, in advance of offering me higher rank and position within Starfleet.

While I appreciated the value of what he was offering, this promotion and its attendant assignment was being driven by politics. . . . I've never been good at politics. Just the same, as the admiral said he still considered me the best officer for the job, my decision to accept or decline—clearly a difficult choice for me—was not one I desired to make quickly. But Admiral Quinn wanted my answer soon. I gave it to him that very night.

While it is quite extraordinary for a Starfleet officer to decline an advancement, especially to flag rank, it is indeed rare that one would at once refuse both a promotion and a prestigious assignment. My decision to decline Admiral Quinn's proposal was guided by a Starfleet officer's first duty—to the truth, whether it involves a scientific, historical, or personal matter. In this particular instance, the personal truth is that while I hold high regard for the mission of Starfleet Academy, I will best serve Admiral Quinn and Starfleet as captain of the *Enterprise*. This is where I belong, at least for the time being. Remaining firm in my decision, I still felt the necessity to tell my old friend that should he ever *really* need me at his side . . . he only need ask.

While I'm confident that my decision to decline Admiral Quinn's offer was correct, I feel it my personal duty to make a contribution to the Academy even as I continue to command the Federation's flagship. In this regard, I can see no better way to fulfill my responsibility to the Academy than preparing this book of thoughts on leadership for the leadership training of future cadets. And it is my sincere hope that this volume will be used as a guide not only by officers in the Starfleet but by civilian leaders in the Federation as well.

Since an officer is rarely more effective than the capabilities of those around him allow, it is my firm belief that very high on the list of an officer's principal duties is the responsibility to develop the leadership abilities of his subordinates. In keeping with this belief, it is my desire to provide you with a resource that addresses leadership qualities that have stood the test of time. I am confident that these qualities will remain cardinal skills of effective leaders, even as you study this record far into the future.

As you progress through this book, I advise you to listen closely to its message. In it, you will find expository illustrations of events during which these leadership qualities were manifest, misapplied, or even neglected. I will record and comment on these events shortly after they have taken place, while they are still fresh in my mind. Indeed, I will record them in the form of journal entries, which are longer and more comprehensive than the log entries that make up the daily record of a starship's progress. But in its final form, this book will be compiled nonlinearly, according to the importance of the leadership qualities it illustrates and discusses, rather than the chronological order in which its recorded events occurred.

As a newly commissioned officer, it is quite ordinary to imitate great leaders you have come to know through your studies and service. But when you stop imitating others and start leading in your own way, you will begin to emerge as a great leader in your own right. To that end, I leave it to each one of you to investigate all possibilities for best employing these lessons in the performance of your various duties as a Starfleet officer. Make it so.

Background

"Jean-Luc Picard"

Superintendent's note. *To learn from the past, we must first know those people who played pivotal roles in our history. To anticipate a better future, we must first know those people who will lead us toward the best that we may become.*

Admiral Andrea Brand
Superintendent, Starfleet Academy

Captain's personal journal: Stardate 48811.5.
At Starfleet Academy.

I began writing this journal midway through my first year as captain of the Federation's flagship, the *U.S.S. Enterprise*-D, and now end it in my eighth year of command. Sadly, the Federation, my crew, and I have all suffered a great loss, as the *Starship Enterprise* has been destroyed on Veridian III. Nevertheless, perhaps it is possible that the *Enterprise*'s crew and their experiences will live forever through the medium of this record that I now turn over to my good friend, Admiral Andrea Brand, to publish for use in leadership training at Starfleet Academy. I am now anxiously waiting to discuss my future role with leaders of Starfleet and the Federation. I only hope that I can continue to serve in a capacity that will allow me to make a difference.

As I fully realize that many of you who will come to read this book may not have a knowledge of who I am, perhaps it would be worthwhile to tell you something of my past in order that you may better understand me.

I was born on Earth in the year 2305 in LaBarre, France, to Maurice and Yvette Gessard Picard. They named me, their second son, Jean-Luc. Mother was a kind, patient, and understanding woman. Fortunately, she was able to see past my weaknesses and nurture my strengths. Father was a tradition-bound vintner, who avoided the use of modern technology whenever possible, as he believed its use would lead to the erosion of those values we should hold most precious. True to his convictions, he relied on conventional methods to produce his celebrated Château Picard wine.

My father and I never understood one another. He neither gave his personal approval of my fascination for space nor encouraged my interest in science. Father wanted me to become a vintner, remain at home, and join him and my brother in the family business. But the simple truth is that I never aspired to pursue the expectations my father held for his sons, and my career interests simply took a different direction. Perhaps this is the reason why I cannot help believing that my father never forgave me for the disappointment I caused him when I left home to attend Starfleet Academy.

My elder brother, Robert, was as tradition-bound as our father. Robert married a wonderful woman, Marie, and they took over the operation of our family vineyard upon Father's death. During our youth, Robert often bullied me and was jealous and resentful of even the least of my achievements. Consequently, our relationship remained one marred by senseless sibling rivalry rather than being one bonded by brotherly love until we had the opportunity to make amends many years later. Although I am particularly grateful for this reconciliation, one that occurred just four years ago, I am deeply saddened to have recently learned that Robert and René, his eleven-year-old son, met an untimely and tragic death, having been burned in a fire. Indeed, their loss leaves virtually no one to carry on the Picard family name, as I have never married or fathered a child.

I was admitted to Starfleet Academy in 2323, at the age of eighteen. My years there were both challenging and enjoyable. As a cadet, I was enthusiastic, and my creative use of enthusiasm sometimes resulted in my being called to the superintendent's office to discuss certain problems—problems our Betazoid superintendent fully understood in advance. These problems notwithstanding, I did form excellent relationships with several instructors, and staff, two in particular. As well as being an extremely capable instructor, Professor Richard Galen is perhaps the most prominent archaeologist of our time. We had a close relationship. I had a father, but Professor Galen was like a father who understood me. He had children, but they didn't follow in his footsteps, and I was like a son who understood him. And I cannot forget Boothby, a groundskeeper. While a cadet, I thought him to be little more than a mean-spirited, vicious old man. I now consider him to be one of the wisest men I have ever known. It was he who helped me right a serious wrong I committed while a cadet—a problem I need not now reveal. Quite simply, Boothby knew that I understood what had to be done to correct this problem and made sure I did just that. I didn't speak to him for months afterward, and have yet to properly thank him for his help. Nevertheless, I must admit that without Boothby's timely intervention, I would not have been allowed to graduate.

Because I was an accomplished wrestler and won the Starfleet Academy marathon on Danula II as a freshman, my sense is that some of my classmates and instructors considered me a capable, all-around athlete. True enough, but perhaps I am better remembered by them as a student scholar, because even though I failed to gain admission to the Academy on my first attempt, I graduated with top honors in my class.

I take no pride in revealing that as a newly commissioned ensign, I was intelligent but not yet wise. Arrogant, cocky, and occasionally lacking proper personal discipline, I had a rather large ego and bountiful self-confidence—too bountiful on at least one occasion.

Shortly after graduating from the Academy, I was on shore leave with Ensigns Marta Batanides and Corey Zweller—two of my classmates—at Starbase Earhart, where we were awaiting our first deep-space assignments. We spent some of this idle time relaxing and playing *dom-jot* at the Bonestell Recreation Facility—a seamy bar and gathering place for all sorts of galactic riffraff.

One evening, after defeating several other Bonestell patrons at *dom-jot,* Ensign Zweller was challenged to a match by a particularly contemptible Nausicaan who was spoiling for a fight. The Nausicaan cheated. Corey lost. Later that evening, when he found out the Nausicaan had cheated, Corey wanted revenge. I helped avenge my friend's loss by helping him rig the table so that the Nausicaan couldn't cheat in a rematch. They played a second time. Corey won. Neither the Nausicaan nor his two friends took kindly to losing. They were outraged and wanted a fight. So I gave them one.

Giving no regard to their physical advantage—the Nausicaans were all nearly twice my size—I took on their leader. Striking him with a double-fisted uppercut to his chin, I knocked the Nausicaan to the floor. A second Nausicaan then attacked me from behind, but I was able to throw him to the floor as well. In the meantime, their leader had gotten up and taken a position behind me. Suddenly and violently, he stabbed me in the back with a long, serrated-edged blade. Passing completely through my body, the knife pierced my heart. I was immediately transported to a nearby medical facility where—the wound being beyond repair—a cardiac replacement was necessary in order to save my life. Had this incident not occurred so near a medical facility, I would have surely died.

My lack of judgment in choosing to take on these despicable but insignificant ruffians proved to be a very hard and painful lesson in self-discipline and ego control. Indeed, it was a difficult lesson that I hope you don't learn in a similar way.

Early in my career, I had the unique opportunity to interact with several prominent leaders who were key figures in shaping the Federation in its formative years. Perhaps most noteworthy among these leaders was Sarek, the Vulcan ambassador to the Federation. Extraordinarily skilled as a diplomat, Ambassador Sarek effected several important peace treaties between the Federation and hostile governments. I learned many valuable things through my acquaintance with him.

As a young officer I was also ambitious, and for ambitious Starfleet officers there are certain costs involved. Such was the case when I became attracted to a lovely young woman, Jenice. Our relationship grew to the point of decision as to our future together. Thinking I must be cautious of long-term commitments that could interfere with my career, I abruptly ended further involvement with her. I now understand fully that even the most ambitious among us cannot be devoted entirely to the sole pursuit of the rewards being a

Starfleet officer affords and still maintain proper balance in life.

Regretfully, I learned this lesson too late to do anything to restore my relationship with Jenice, and the lack of closure with her left me unsettled for a good while. In the meantime, my passions for astrophysics, music, archaeology, riding Arabian mares, and drama filled the void created by Jenice's absence and provided me welcome relief from the pressures of my official duties.

As a lieutenant, I served as a bridge officer aboard the *U.S.S. Stargazer*. During a hostile engagement, our ship's captain was mortally wounded. I took immediate charge of our vessel and ordered a counterattack. My initiative and actions saved both the *Stargazer* and its remaining crew. Starfleet Command rewarded me with a three-grade promotion—to the rank of captain—and gave me my first command. Despite this promotion and its attending billet coming about through tragedy, I still consider it an honor to have been selected to command the *Stargazer* and replace a leader I greatly admired.

I had been captain of the *Stargazer* for approximately twenty years when we neared the Zeta Maxia System and came under attack by an unidentified Threat force, later identified as Ferengi. During this brutal engagement, the *Stargazer* was virtually destroyed, but not before we inflicted heavy damage on the Threat vessel. This counterstrike came about as the result of my spontaneous decision to momentarily accelerate to warp speed, which, from the Threat force's perspective, caused our spacecraft to appear to be in two places simultaneously. This tactic—now acclaimed as the "Picard Maneuver"—confused our attackers and allowed us to fire on them. The damage to the Ferengi spacecraft was sufficient to allow the *Stargazer*'s surviving crew and me to board a shuttlecraft and escape certain death.

In accordance with standard Starfleet policy governing the loss of a starship, I was court-martialed over this incident. As expected, justice prevailed. I was exonerated of all charges brought against me.

In 2363, at the age of fifty-eight, and some thirty-six years after graduating from Starfleet Academy, it was my distinct honor and privilege to be named captain of NCC-1701-D, the fifth starship named *Enterprise*. As is the case for all its predecessors, the *Enterprise* is the Federation's flagship for deep-space exploration, scientific research, diplomatic and trade missions, and defensive operations.

The Federation places high value on competent leadership, as do I. For this reason, I was particularly gratified by the high caliber of the officers who comprised my key staff aboard the *Enterprise*. Frankly, they were among the very best in Starfleet.

Midway through my first year as captain of the *Starship Enterprise,* those officers serving with me on the main bridge were: Commander William Riker, my Number One and second-in-command; Lieutenant Commander Data, my second officer and operations manager; Lieutenant Natasha Yar, chief of security— who was killed during a rescue mission on Vagra II; Lieutenant Junior Grade Worf, flight control officer; and Lieutenant Junior Grade Geordi La Forge, our flight controller. I was also joined in command of the *Enterprise* by Deanna Troi, ship's counselor; and Dr. Beverly Crusher, who served as our chief medical officer, excepting a one-year leave of absence while she served as chief of Starfleet Medical. At the time when the *Enterprise* was destroyed, Mr. La Forge was serving as our chief engineer and Mr. Worf as our chief of security. All others remained in their initial assignments.

I

Focus

"Mission"

Superintendent's foreword to "Focus." *The U.S.S. Enterprise-D's captain was one who led by consensus, but who was also confident in taking decisive, independent decisions wherever and whenever appropriate or necessary. As is the case for other senior officers, Jean-Luc Picard constantly struggled with competing demands for his time and attention. Despite these demands, Captain Picard could immediately separate mission priorities from other important issues or less significant problems. It is precisely this attribute to focus that allowed Captain Picard to use his time and effort on activities and matters of priority. It was also this quality that caused Jean-Luc Picard to excel as captain of the Federation's flagship. In addition, as he held high expectations for his crew, Captain Picard took every opportunity to instill this leadership attribute in them as well.*

Aboard the Enterprise, *Captain Picard and his crew*

enjoyed both novel distractions and leisurely diversions from the often intense strain of their duties and assignments. Nonetheless, while on duty, the captain and crew of the Enterprise *had sufficient self-discipline to put aside anything or anyone who would divert their concentration from their primary responsibilities. In a word, Captain Picard and his crew were "focused."*

Admiral Andrea Brand
Superintendent, Starfleet Academy

Captain's personal journal: Stardate 44019.3. Departing Earth.

We were recently subjected to a most horrifying experience. Indeed, one meted on the Federation by none other than the Borg of the galaxy's Delta Quadrant. An immensely robust and resilient race of humanoids who exhibit a high degree of intelligence and adaptability in their tactics, the Borg are enhanced with surgically implanted cybernetic devices, which provide each of them with extraordinary technical and combat capabilities. Some are equipped with different, special-purpose cybernetic devices; however, the Borg are linked to a *collective consciousness* by a highly sophisticated subspace network, which provides them all with constant supervision and direction. As they function interdependently but with *one mind,* the *individual* doesn't exist within their society, not even in concept. Formidable foes indeed, the Borg are known to have assimilated entire races into their collective, and their venture into Federation space was for none other than the purpose of assimilating the human race.

Although this experience placed a heavy toll on the Federation, it also exacted a heavy price from me. It is only after taking shore leave to my familial home in LaBarre, France, that I am now able to write about it. Despite the tragedy that occurred during this experience, it is one rich in examples of an officer's need to stay focused.

The *Enterprise* responded to a distress call from one of the Federation's outermost colonies, the New Providence colony on Jouret IV. On arrival, our sensors could not detect any life signs on the planet's surface. Commander Riker led an away team to investigate. Transporting to the planet's surface, the away team discovered that every building, all equipment, and all vegetation had been obliterated. None of the nine hundred colonists were to be found.

Based on my initial report of the away team's dreadful discovery, Starfleet believed the destruction of the New Providence colony to be the work of the Borg. As such, they immediately sent Admiral Hanson, who directed Starfleet Tactical's initiatives, to develop a defense against the Borg, and Lieutenant Commander Shelby, who had been in charge of Borg tactical analysis for the past six months, to assist us with further investigation.

Upon their arrival, Admiral Hanson and Commander Shelby briefed Commander Riker and me. Starfleet had known for over a year that the Borg were approaching Federation space. Every available resource had been committed to developing a defense against them.

Nevertheless, the defense strategy was still under development, new weapons were still in the design stage. As such, the Federation was not ready to defend itself against a Borg attack.

Confirmation that the Borg had destroyed the New Providence colony would require further analysis of Jouret IV's surface. But as it would be dark soon, additional investigation would have to wait until daybreak. Commander Riker set the away team's departure time for eight o'clock the following morning. Commander Shelby would join the away team for this mission. That decided, Commander Riker showed Commander Shelby to her guest quarters.

Admiral Hanson then informed me that Starfleet had extended Commander Riker an invitation to command the *U.S.S. Melbourne.* I knew Will had turned down command of starships on two previous occasions, yet I was unaware of this new offer. Admiral Hanson noted that Starfleet was becoming impatient with Mr. Riker. If he refused this promotion, others, now junior to him, would soon pass him by. The admiral thought Lieutenant Commander Shelby would be an ideal replacement for Mr. Riker and suggested I give Will some career advice—accept Starfleet's offer.

The following morning, Commander Riker and Mr. La Forge arrived at the transporter room, where Chief O'Brien informed them that Commander Shelby had taken Data with her and already transported to the planet's surface. Mr. Riker was not pleased with her initiative.

By the time Will and Geordi arrived on Jouret IV, Commander Shelby and Data had already found evidence that the destruction of the New Providence colony was unmistakably the work of the Borg. With the Borg confirmed to have entered Federation space, Admiral Hanson returned to Starbase 324 to discuss strategy with others at Starfleet Command. Commander Shelby remained on board the *Enterprise* to help us with tactical preparations.

Commander Riker briefed me on the actions he had taken in light of the Borg threat. After which, I asked Will what he thought of Commander Shelby. Will said she seemed competent but needed supervision. She took the initiative a little too easily, even in risky situations.

I went on to ask Will why he had not accepted command of the *Melbourne* and was still on the *Enterprise*. Misinterpreting my line of questioning as an indication that I might be trying to get rid of him, Will said, while keeping his career plans to himself, that he had decided to turn down Starfleet's offer. The *Melbourne* was a fine ship in her own right, but she was just not the *Enterprise*. For the present, he was quite satisfied to be serving as my first officer. Besides, with the Borg present in Federation space, I needed him now more than ever. I agreed, but as Starfleet also needed good captains at the moment, I urged Will to reconsider his decision.

The next morning, Admiral Hanson gave us some very disturbing news over the viewscreen. During the previous night, Starbase 157 received a distress call from the *U.S.S. Lalo,* which reported contact with a cube-shaped alien vessel near Zeta Alpha II.

There had been no contact with the *Lalo* since. Admiral Hanson's report confirmed our worst fear: the Borg were continuing their attack on the Federation. With Admiral Hanson in command, the Federation was coming to meet them with every available starship. As the *Enterprise* was the Federation starship nearest to Zeta Alpha II, we were to keep the Borg occupied until help arrived, which would be at least six days.

We set course for Zeta Alpha II, and shortly thereafter Mr. Worf reported that sensors had detected an unidentified spacecraft. Moments later, we were within visual range. To no one's surprise, the object that appeared on the screen was a Borg ship—an exceptionally powerful and well-armed colossal cube-shaped vessel just like the one we had seen, and boarded, near System J-25 when Q first introduced us to them. I instructed Mr. Worf to dispatch a subspace message to Admiral Hanson informing him that we had engaged the Borg.

As warning alarms sounded, Worf informed me that the Borg were hailing me by name. On the screen, they ordered me to lower our shields and transport myself aboard their vessel. Otherwise, they would destroy the *Enterprise.*

We were puzzled by the Borg demands, but unwilling to comply with them. I informed the Borg that we had developed new technology since our last meeting and were prepared to use it if they didn't leave Federation space. Just as I had ignored their demands, the Borg ignored my warning. A brief battle ensued, but the *Enterprise* was no match for the Borg ship and we had to run for our lives.

We entered the Paulson Nebula, a dense astronomical cloud rich in dilithium hydroxyls, magnesium, and chromium—materials that cause interference with sensor functions. It offered us a temporary safe haven. I still had no idea why the Borg were showing so much interest in either me or the *Enterprise*. Regardless, they waited outside as we remained safely inside the Paulson Nebula, where my staff continued making preparations to do battle with them.

Commander Shelby recommended to Mr. Riker that we separate the *Enterprise*'s saucer from her battle section. Doing so would create two targets for the Borg and, where there was now one, there would be two spacecraft to attack the Borg. Commander Riker thought this tactic was too great a risk.

While Mr. Riker set about other duties, Commander Shelby came to my ready room, where she informed me of her recommendation. Going around one's superior officer to make certain that one's voice is heard is not done aboard the *Enterprise*. This may explain why my first officer was noticeably irritated to find Commander Shelby with me when he came to report on the progress of our preparations. I agreed with Mr. Riker that Commander Shelby's plan was too risky at the time, but told him that he should consider it as a fallback position.

The *Enterprise* began to rock intermittently as

the Borg ship randomly fired magnetometric guided charges into the nebula. After one of the charges hit our ship, I realized that the dense cloud was no longer a safe haven, and I ordered the *Enterprise* out of the nebula. The Borg ship gave chase, and within a few moments had its tractor beam locked on to us.

Our shields soon lost all power and a Borg beamed aboard the bridge. Worf immediately fired his phaser at the Borg, killing him instantly. Then a second Borg beamed onto the bridge. This one deflected Worf's phaser fire because the Borg had quickly adapted their body shields to deflect our phasers' modified frequency. Commander Riker attempted to wrestle the Borg, which quickly proved futile. Then Worf attacked the Borg, only to be knocked to the deck. Suddenly, a third Borg beamed aboard. This one came up behind me and injected me with a sedative, and the Borg promptly beamed back to their ship, taking me with them.

The Borg immediately disengaged their tractor beam and set a direct course for Sector 001—Earth and the heart of Federation space. Under way, the Borg informed me that they wished to improve themselves by adding human biological and technological distinctiveness to their own. Human culture would be adapted to service them. I argued with the Borg to no effect.

Moreover, they considered human culture to be archaic and authority-driven. As I was the captain of the strongest ship in the Federation, they thought me to be an authority figure, one who often spoke for my people and one to whom my people would listen. This explained why they had come after me. Indeed, the Borg had chosen me to introduce them to the human race.

Despite my attempts to resist, I was taken to a medical bay, where my captors began surgically transforming me into one of them. In the process, the Borg neurologically connected me with their collective consciousness, which also allowed them to assimilate everything I knew.

Meanwhile, the *Enterprise* followed the Borg ship. Her weapons systems had been reconfigured to concentrate all energy through the main deflector, which would generate an enormous charge—one sufficient to destroy the Borg ship. However, there was a problem. This modified weapon could only be fired at impulse speed. This meant that the *Enterprise*'s crew had to find a way to get the Borg ship to drop out of warp. Moreover, as I later learned, they had not given up on the idea of rescuing me.

To these ends, an away team was to beam aboard the Borg ship. Based on previous experience, my crew knew that their presence on the ship would be ignored as long as they posed no threat. They would have to act quickly. The away team planned to disrupt the Borg ship's power systems, which would cause it to drop out of warp speed. They would find me, then transport us back to the *Enterprise* before the Borg could react. If this phase of their strategy succeeded, the *Enterprise*'s modified weapon would then be fired at the collective's ship.

With Commander Shelby as its leader, the away team

succeeded in destroying several power-distribution nodes on the Borg ship, killing a few Borg in the process. However, further destruction was prevented when the Borg adapted to the new frequency modifications the away team had made to their phasers. This also meant the away team was no longer safe aboard the Borg ship. As they prepared to transport back to the *Enterprise,* the away team got a startling glimpse of the new me.

Just as the away team arrived back on the *Enterprise* and reported their discovery to Commander Riker, I hailed my former shipmates. On the screen, I relayed this message: "I am Locutus of Borg. Resistance is futile. Your life, as it has been, is over. From this time forward, you will service us."

Under the circumstances, Commander Riker had to act without delay, before the Borg could repair their ship and resume warp speed. As such, Will ordered Worf to fire. But the tremendous blast of energy generated by the *Enterprise*'s modified weapons systems had no impact on the collective's spacecraft. Over the viewscreen, I informed Commander Riker why. My knowledge and experience were now part of the Borg, which had allowed them to adapt their ship's shields sufficiently to absorb the *Enterprise*'s new weapon.

As soon as the Borg ship's power systems were repaired, we resumed course toward Earth at warp speed. Along the way, the Borg continued making cybernetic enhancements to me.

As anticipated, the blast burned out the *Enterprise*'s main navigational deflector and damaged her shields and reactor core. Repairs would take eight to twelve hours. For the time being, the *Enterprise* could not pursue the Borg ship. Commander Riker and my senior staff reported this incident to Admiral Hanson. The admiral informed them that the Federation's fleet was headed to intercept the Borg ship at system Wolf 359. In addition, the Klingons were sending ships and the Federation was even considering asking the Romulans to help. As he now considered me a casualty of war, Admiral Hanson gave Commander Riker a field commission to the rank of captain and placed him in command of the *Enterprise*. Captain Riker was reluctantly forced to appoint Lieutenant Commander Shelby as his first officer, giving her a field promotion to the rank of full commander. His reluctance had less to do with her capabilities, which were exceptional, than it did with the fact that there were others perhaps more qualified to become the *Enterprise*'s executive officer. However, under the circumstances, it was just not a time for major changes in staff assignments.

The Borg approached Wolf 359 and were met by the Federation's armada. Make no mistake about it, having the benefit of my knowledge of the Federation's defensive and offensive capabilities, the Borg wasted no time in devastating thirty-nine of the forty starships sent to intercept them, killing some eleven thousand of the Federation's people in the process. I cannot find adequate words to express the grief this has caused me. Quite simply, it was a tragic loss, one in which Locutus of Borg played a pivotal role.

Will Riker has since told me that after all repairs

were made to the *Enterprise,* he ordered a course for Wolf 359. Under way, while the senior staff continued working on alternate tactics to deal with the Borg, Captain Riker returned to his ready room. He was thinking about what I would do in this situation, when Guinan paid him a visit, the purpose of which was to advise Will to let go of me. She told him that the only way he could defeat the Borg was to stop thinking about what I would do and come up with his own plans. The Borg had assimilated my knowledge; if he continued to follow the manner in which I had taught him, the *Enterprise* would surely be defeated.

As they approached Wolf 359, the crew of the *Enterprise* bore witness to the mass destruction that had taken place. Soon after, their sensors detected the wake the Borg ship left as it continued toward Earth, and set a course after it. Captain Riker ordered Commander Shelby to prepare to initiate her plan to separate the saucer section from the *Enterprise.* Commander Shelby reminded Captain Riker that I had been briefed on this alternative—the Borg would be prepared for it. Mr. Riker already knew this to be the case. He was counting on it.

The *Enterprise* closed within communications range of the Borg ship and hailed me—Locutus of Borg. Captain Riker said he wanted to end the hostilities. As such, he wanted to meet and discuss our terms.

As Locutus, I remarked to Number One that he was not about to discuss terms of a surrender. Rather, he was attempting to deceive me. Captain Riker told Locutus that if the Borg were in possession of all

Captain Picard's knowledge, then Locutus would know that Mr. Riker never lied to his commanding officer. Locutus then informed Mr. Riker that discussion was irrelevant. Captain Riker was to disarm the *Enterprise*'s weapons and escort us to Sector 001, where the Borg would begin assimilating human culture and technology.

The Borg had adapted their ship's electromagnetic field, which blocked the *Enterprise*'s main transporter function. This being so, Data and Worf were then given orders to initiate a contingency plan.

Captain Riker asked Locutus for more time to prepare his people for assimilation. I told Number One that preparation was irrelevant. His attempt at delay would not succeed. The human race would be assimilated as easily as Picard had been. At that point, I informed Number One that the Borg ship was going on to Earth. If he attempted to intervene, his ship would be destroyed. Mr. Riker shouted back words to the effect that we should take our best shot. The *Enterprise* was about to intervene.

No sooner was that said than Commander Shelby separated the *Enterprise*'s saucer and launched an attack on the Borg ship. In the battle section, Captain Riker simultaneously began evasive maneuvers as the Borg ship attempted lock on, completely ignoring the saucer section.

Commander Shelby fired an antimatter spread at the Borg ship—a tactic intended to mask the launch of a shuttle from the *Enterprise*'s battle section. Data and Worf were on board the shuttle and attempting to penetrate the Borg ship's electromagnetic field, when the shuttle's engine ionization discharge was detected by the collective. The Borg immediately redeployed their tractor beam to lock on to the approaching shuttle. Will promptly ordered Data to cut the shuttle's engine and continue unpowered, which allowed the shuttle to complete its penetration of the electromagnetic field without further detection.

Once inside the perimeter of the electromagnetic field, Data and Worf used the shuttle's escape transporter to beam aboard the Borg ship. After a brief battle with several Borg, Worf injected me with a sedative, whereupon Data and he beamed back to the shuttle, taking me with them. Fortunately, before the Borg destroyed the shuttle, we had already beamed back to the *Enterprise*.

As Captain Riker maneuvered the battle section to dock with the saucer, the Borg changed heading and resumed course toward Earth. And as soon as her sections were rejoined, the *Enterprise* resumed pursuit.

I was taken to sickbay, where Dr. Crusher made a diagnosis of my condition. While she was determined to undo what the Borg had done to me, Captain Riker's more immediate priority was to find out if I possessed information about Borg vulnerabilities. If so, he wanted to find a way to extract this information from me.

Upon examination, Data detected a set of interactive, complex subspace signals that were allowing me to communicate with the collective, and correctly hypothesized these transmissions were the basis for the

Borg's collective consciousness. Beverly told Will and Data that blocking my interactive communication with the Borg ship might very well cause me to self-destruct. Therefore, Will ruled out this option. For the time being, he wanted Locutus of Borg to remain alive.

Dr. Crusher knew that with my interactive transmission with the Borg cut off, she could remove my cybernetic implants. However, so long as the implants continued to function, she could not separate the man in Locutus from his machine. Data then suggested that perhaps there was a way he could help access the machine in Locutus.

In sickbay, I continued to tell the staff that they would all soon become one with the Borg; they should not resist. Once assimilated, the quality of their lives would improve. Suddenly, Dr. Crusher came up to my side and injected me with a sedative and Data carried me to his laboratory.

Meanwhile, Commander Shelby hailed Captain Riker and informed him that the Borg ship had entered Sector 001. Captain Riker immediately returned to the bridge. Once there, Commander Shelby told him that the Borg ship had dropped out of warp. She also said that planetary defenses were prepared, but against the Borg there was little hope of success.

Data was able to make a connection between his android brain and my cybernetic modifications. Through this connection Data discovered that the Borg group consciousness is divided into subcommands, which is a necessary division in order for them to carry out all functions. Continuing to process information about the Borg, Data was informing the others in his lab that Borg defense, communication, and navigation were controlled by a root command implanted into each . . . when I received instruction from the collective to disrupt the experiment. I unsucessfully attempted to destroy the neurolink connection. Dr. Crusher reported to Data that her monitors were showing a sudden and rapid increase in my neurological activity. The crew surmised that the Borg were beginning to cut off their link with me. Data quickly checked the computer control panel and found my subspace signal connection with the collective to be unchanged. Thus, whatever was causing the rapid increase in Locutus's neuroactivity was unclear.

Counselor Troi had been observing the procedure and sensed the cause of the increase in Locutus's neuroactivity to be an attempt by me to break through my altered state and communicate with them. Excited by the prospects of my reemergence, Deanna reported to Captain Riker that Data had just made first contact with Captain Picard!

From the bridge, Captain Riker asked Data if he was able to communicate with me. Data reported that as he had not yet been able to create a neuropath around the Borg implant, Captain Picard had initiated communication with him.

Captain Riker then received an updated situation report. The Borg had halted their approach toward Earth, and the *Enterprise* was two minutes and four seconds away from intercept. Mr. Riker thought aloud that the Borg must be worried as they knew the

Enterprise's crew had accessed their collective consciousness.

Data told Captain Riker that it was uncertain whether the Borg were unwilling or unable to terminate their subspace link with me. On hearing Data's comments, Dr. Crusher quickly, and correctly, arrived at the notion that this could be the Borg's Achilles' heel. The Borg functioned with *total* interdependence, thinking and acting as one mind. As I was now part of their collective consciousness, cutting me off was impossible for them. It would be like asking one of the crew to cut off one of their limbs—they just wouldn't be able to do it.

Hypothesizing that what one did, all of the Borg would do, Will asked Data if it was possible to plant a command into the Borg consciousness. Data said it was a possibility, but would require altering the pathway from the root command to instruct all of the branch points in their collective consciousness. Captain Riker ordered Data to attempt to make the necessary alterations. Data confirmed that he would, but wanted to know what command to implant. Captain Riker told him to choose something simple.

As Data was making the alterations, the Borg ship increased power and maneuvered toward the *Enterprise*. Captain Riker ordered a red alert. The Borg ship overpowered the *Enterprise* once again. The Borg ship's shields deflected the *Enterprise*'s fire, while its fire inflicted heavy damage to the *Enterprise*. And, within moments, its tractor beam had locked on to the *Enterprise*.

Captain Riker signaled Data to see what progress he had made. Data had not yet been able to complete the alterations, which meant that he had not yet been able to plant a simple command into the Borg consciousness. Will was not willing to go down easily. He ordered Wesley to set a collision course directly at the Borg ship. Geordi was to prepare the *Enterprise* for warp speed. Simply speaking, if the *Enterprise* was going down anyway, she was going to take as many of the Borg with her as possible.

Back in Data's lab, I—Jean-Luc Picard—understood that he was attempting to implant a destructive computer command into the Borg collective consciousness. Nevertheless, Data hadn't determined what this command should be, so I struggled to communicate such a command to him. But, as I was semiconscious myself, all I could bring myself to say was, "Sleep. Sleep. Sleep, Data."

Data knew what to do next.

The Borg assault on the *Enterprise* continued. They had just activated their ship's cutting beam when Data hailed Captain Riker and told him to be belay the plan to collide with the Borg ship to give him more time.

Simultaneously, the Borg intensified their attack and were inflicting heavy damage to the *Enterprise*. As the computer voiced a warning that the *Enterprise*'s outer hull had been breached, Worf asked Captain Riker if he should activate the evacuation sequence. Will told him "negative" and signaled Data for his final report. Data asked Captain Riker to stand by; however, the ship's computer was giving a verbal warning that the inner hull was about to be breached, which would cause the *Enterprise* to decompress.

Suddenly, the Borg ceased their attack. Captain Riker hailed Data and asked, "What the hell happened, Data?"

Data reported that he had successfully implanted a message in the Borg collective consciousness, which had misdirected them into believing that it was time to regenerate. In effect, Data had told them to "go to sleep."

Worf reported the Borg ship's power drive to be operating at a minimal level; its electromagnetic field had been disengaged. Captain Riker directed Commander Shelby to take an away team to the Borg ship to confirm that they were indeed sleeping and then made his way to Data's laboratory.

Commander Shelby confirmed that the Borg were sleeping, but her away team's tricorder readings were fluctuating rapidly, indicating that the Borg ship's power link was about to feed back on itself. Indeed, Data's command had caused the Borg ship to malfunction and start a self-destruction sequence. Commander Shelby asked Captain Riker if he wanted her away team to attempt to stop it. Will instructed her to stand by.

Dr. Crusher informed Captain Riker that there was no way to tell what the destruction of the Borg ship would do to me. Data also suggested that it might be an opportune time to examine the Borg and their ship more closely. Captain Riker disagreed.

Ordering Data to disconnect his neurolink from me, Captain Riker told the away team to return to the

Enterprise. As soon as the away team was back aboard, Ensign Crusher was to move the *Enterprise* to a safe distance away from the Borg ship. Captain Riker's decisive action came just in time. No sooner was the *Enterprise* at a safe distance than the Borg ship self-destructed in a massive explosion.

I survived the Borg self-destruction and immediately regained full consciousness of my real self. Still, I remembered everything that had happened, including Number One's brilliantly executed, but rather unorthodox, strategy to implant a destructive computer command into the Borg collective consciousness.

Commander Shelby was ordered back to Starfleet Command, where she would help supervise the rebuilding of the fleet and defense systems. The *Enterprise* proceeded to Earth Station McKinley, where she and I would undergo extensive repairs.

Captain's personal journal: Observations on "Focus." Stardate: 44075.1. En route to Ogus II.

The Federation was unprepared for the Borg invasion. This was due not to lack of effort but to lack of time. Indeed, the Borg invaded our space long before their arrival was anticipated, and it became necessary to answer their challenge with inventiveness and courage.

Although I am truly saddened by the death and destruction the Borg inflicted upon the Federation, I feel that we ultimately defeated them because my key staff stayed focused on matters of immediate consequence while operating in a veritable sea of potential confusion. Other issues, less important than defeating the Borg, also came into play during the course of this encounter.

On reflection, this crisis situation was an inappropriate time to be entertaining discussions of changes in either Commander Riker's or Lieutenant Commander Shelby's assignment. Indeed, a change in a starship's first officer requires time. The new Number One has to adapt to a new role—possibly on a new ship and with an unfamiliar crew—and the crew has to become accustomed to interacting with whoever assumes the first officer's role. Moreover, Commander Shelby had not completed her work with Borg tactical analysis, and her expertise was needed at Starfleet Command.

It is also true that Starfleet Command had offered command of the *Melbourne* to Mr. Riker before the Borg entered Federation space, but once they had, it would have been best to put this offer on hold for the time being. Even so, Admiral Hanson had high regard for Lieutenant Commander Shelby and wasted no time in recommending her as Will's replacement—should he accept Starfleet's offer. Obviously, Admiral Hanson had discussed with Commander Shelby Mr. Riker's pending promotion—and that he was going to recommend her as Will's replacement—before they arrived on board the *Enterprise*. She made every attempt to prove herself to be the right choice for the job, which was distracting and presumptuous. However, despite Commander Shelby's risk taking and overtures to impress, she remained focused on her primary assignment. As experience has taught me, such behavior is quite normal for highly talented and confident officers, and it often becomes necessary to find a way to bridle their need to impress without suppressing their enthusiasm and passion for their duties.

To be sure, Commander Riker was faced with difficult decisions and objectives including defeating the Borg while effecting my rescue. Indeed, while he eventually succeeded, it was not without the collaboration of the entire crew, who presented him with several options and total support. Counseled by Guinan to forget everything I had taught him—or be destroyed—Mr. Riker showed his inventiveness by way of a strategy that I didn't anticipate. Appointed to command the *Enterprise* during a time of crisis, Captain Riker had to make a key staffing decision. Perhaps under normal circumstances Will would have chosen differently, but his choice was wise and received the full support and understanding of the crew.

I cannot ignore Dr. Crusher's and Data's abilities to improvise methods that not only served Mr. Riker's need for information about Borg vulnerabilities but led to the collective's self-destruction while preserving my life in the process. This was not a simple challenge and required simultaneous concentration on several priorities, which could very well have been viewed as competing demands.

As for myself, there was nothing anyone could have done to prevent my abduction, nor was I able to resist what the Borg did to me. There is no denying that Locutus played a role in the destruction that followed the collective's assimilation of my knowledge. But make no mistake about it: Jean-Luc Picard never abandoned his loyalty for the Federation, nor did I ever lose faith in my crew.

Captain's personal journal: Lessons on "Focus." Stardate 44084.9. En route to Starbase 416.

Many vital lessons may be drawn from our recent Borg experience. In my mind, focus is the cardinal quality of an effective officer. For this reason, I suggest that you give thoughtful consideration to these lessons.

- To be effective, an officer must have unclouded vision about what is ahead. Such vision demands that the officer deal with all his priorities, but not necessarily in sequential order. Indeed, an officer must develop the ability to see all ramifications of his action, or inaction, at once.
- An officer's effectiveness is in direct proportion to the degree of focus he applies to the most important of his duties.
- Officers should develop the full mental ability to adapt readily to varied demands and to novel situations, and learn to meet crisis by inventiveness. Such officers become of far greater value to the Starfleet than they would be if they had ceased developing their mental ability once they achieved mere imitative skill.
- The demands others make on an officer for his time and attention increases with rank and

position. However, as one cannot be omnipresent, it becomes vital that an officer quickly distinguish between profitable and wasteful use of his time and presence.

- Clearness and persistence of aim reduce the volume of effort it takes to be effective.
- While being sidetracked may result from overloading oneself with too many responsibilities, gifted officers most often fail because of wasteful or wavering dispersions of their gifts.
- In space, officers can ill afford to allow their crew to become distracted by misdirected competition.
- When one is not manifestly fitted for a job, the best way to become successful at it is by concentrated enthusiasm and devotion.
- The surest way for an officer to be selected for higher position is by concentrating on doing his present job well. Indeed, one who focuses too much concern on what his future may hold loses much of his present self.
- When an officer becomes convinced that the power of concentration leads to mission success, he will take great pains to cultivate this power in his crew, and will prudently and tirelessly guard against wanton dispersions of profitable effort and valuable resources.

And by way of concluding these lessons,

- Concentrating on the most important aspects of one's duties gives all the secondary or mechanical operations of one's efforts the ease and exactness of habit.

Without equivocation, I guarantee that if you first focus your efforts on matters of the highest concern and profit that attend your position, you will set free so much more of your crew's, and your own, initiative, power, innovation, and imagination, all of which are inseparable from mission success. Make it so.

II

Urgency

"Engage"

Superintendent's foreword to "Urgency." *Apathy, laziness, distraction, and interference can all lead to a self-inflicted workplace crisis created by the failure to do what needs to be done within acceptable time limits or according to established standards. Panic—the frantic search for a quick solution—usually follows the realization that a self-inflicted crisis exists.*

At best, one person's procrastination disrupts the work of others. At worst, procrastination undermines productivity, erodes organizational morale, and creates unnecessary workplace stress. Procrastination can hardly become an admirable leadership quality as it is incompatible with the qualities of effective leadership.

Aboard the Enterprise, *important responsibilities were undertaken with a sense of urgency marked by confident resolve and purposeful action. Neither panic nor frenzy attended the urgency with which Captain Picard and his senior staff performed their duties or in how they directed the activities of others of their ship's crew.*

Competently led, the men and women who served aboard the Federation's flagship were people of enthusiastic spirit who had a keen sense of what was urgent and what could wait. Indeed, the officers and crew of the U.S.S. Enterprise *were driven by productive action, wasting neither time nor resources.*

And so, aboard the Enterprise, *whether a new course was set or a new priority identified, the only proper response was—"Engage!"*

Admiral Andrea Brand
Superintendent, Starfleet Academy

Captain's personal journal: Stardate 46690.9. Departing the Remmler Array.

After extended voyages, I am always delighted to grant the crew of the *Enterprise* some well-deserved shore leave and seek restful recreational activity myself. Under normal circumstances, shore leave can be taken without anyone being called back to duty by unexpected emergencies. But, as a recent event illustrates, in space one can never count on normal circumstances and the call to return to duty can be one of great urgency.

We docked the *Enterprise* at the Remmler Array—in orbit around the planet on which Starfleet's Arkaria Base is located—to have the *Enterprise* undergo a routine maintenance procedure to remove accumulated baryon particles from its hull. As living tissue cannot survive exposure to a baryon sweep, it was necessary to totally evacuate the ship—a necessity that gave all of us good reason to take some welcomed shore leave.

Complete evacuation of a starship calls for special precautions such as disabling all command functions, which is rare indeed. Moreover, during the previous five years the *Enterprise* had logged more warp hours than most starships do in ten. As a result, the baryon sweep would require a stronger beam than normal; therefore, Commander La Forge installed additional field diverters to protect the main computer core and key systems located on the bridge.

Prior to evacuating the *Enterprise,* I was met with several urgent matters—including providing Counselor Troi with alternatives to speed up the transport of the crew, their families, and civilian staff to Arkaria Base, suggesting a way for Dr. Crusher to protect some living tissue samples, and authorizing the computer to disable all command functions.

True to a tradition established long ago, I toured my ship to ensure that everyone had evacuated. As captain, I would be the last of the crew to leave the *Enterprise.* Departing the bridge, I noticed the arrival of the several technicians who would complete preparation for the baryon sweep. Little did I realize just then that they had other intentions as well—ones of a criminal nature.

After transporting to Arkaria Base, I went to a reception given by Commander Hutchinson, the base commander, where I was not surprised to find him making his way around the room engaging my staff with small talk. Mr. Hutchinson was sharing some of the planet's more interesting features with us when he happened to mention that the base had horses and that there was a network of riding trails throughout the planet's plains. While Commander Hutchinson thought the cold weather and absence of people along the muddy trails would make riding unpleasant, I thought these conditions to be rather perfect for a relaxing ride.

I asked Mr. La Forge how long we had before the baryon sweep would begin. He told me, "About twenty-five minutes, sir."

It was just enough time for me to return to the ship and get my saddle, which came as an offbeat surprise to Counselor Troi and Commander La Forge. Although they were aware of my love for riding, neither they nor other members of my senior staff had been aware that I kept a saddle aboard the *Enterprise*.

Transporting back to the ship, I went to my quarters, changed into proper riding attire, collected my saddle, and headed back to the transporter room. Along the way, I noticed something odd—an open ODN junction box. As I stooped down to inspect the box, I was approached by a technician, who wanted to know what I was doing. I observed that someone had left the junction box open, and that I thought his crew was supposed to be off the ship once the field diverters were in place. The technician paused and said that the diverters required synchronization before his team could leave. As such, he was laser-bonding a backup link—the laser torch was in his hand. To be sure, I realized I had inadvertently discovered that something taking place aboard the *Enterprise* was very wrong. What the technician had just told me was not standard procedure for installing field diverters.

Sensing the need for caution, I told the technician, "Oh, I see. Well then, I'd better let you finish up so that you can get off the ship."

As I turned to walk away, I heard the technician say, "Excuse me a minute."

Anticipating what he was about to do, I whirled and struck the technician with my saddle just as he was about to attack me with the laser torch. We wrestled briefly before I rendered him unconscious. Just then, the *Enterprise*'s operating lights began to turn off and the computer announced that the auto-shutdown sequence was in progress. Primary power would be off-line in one minute.

I ran toward the transporter room, hoping to have time to transport back to Arkaria Base before primary power went off-line. Along the way I saw two more armed technicians. To avoid them, I diverted from my direct route, which resulted in my arriving at the transporter room too late. Primary power had shut-down. I was now trapped aboard the *Enterprise* facing two immediate dangers, a baryon sweep that would kill me and armed technicians who apparently were just as likely to do the same.

My immediate priority was to find out exactly what was taking place aboard the *Enterprise,* while finding a way back to Arkaria Base. I went back to where I had left the technician and dragged him to sickbay to interrogate him. Once inside sickbay, I secured a hyposyringe filled with a sedative and set my phaser to full power. As I was about to revive him, I heard a call for "Devor" coming over his personal communicator. When Devor failed to respond to her call, I heard Kelsey—the woman I surmised to be hailing the unconscious technician—say that the baryon sweep was interfering with their communicators. Consequently, she ordered someone by the name of Kiros to find the missing technician. They were to meet her and the rest of their party in main engineering.

As the technician regained consciousness, I asked him who he was and what he was doing on my ship. He noticed the phaser I was aiming at him and reminded me that the baryon sweep's high-frequency plasma field wouldn't allow it to function. I told the technician that he was probably right. So I aimed his laser torch at him and said, "But I'd like to bet that this will."

Refusing to answer my questions, the technician said he knew that because I was a Starfleet officer, I wouldn't kill him. There was no point in my interrogating him further. So I used the hypospray to sedate him and was cautiously making my way to main engineering when another armed technician, whom I assumed to be Kiros, captured me.

As I was to learn later, back at the reception Commander La Forge was helping himself to some hors d'oeuvres when he noticed some strange energy readings coming from under the table. Geordi was investigating the source of these readings when Mr. Orton, the station administrator, walked over and asked him if anything was wrong. Geordi told the station administrator about the energy readings, which Orton attempted to dismiss as a malfunctioning heating element. Geordi offered to look at the heating element, but a waiter suddenly approached him and said that they could handle the problem. Then Orton took Geordi by the arm and led away from the table.

Commander Riker had been observing what was taking place and sensed something was wrong. He walked toward the table. The waiter panicked and warned Orton, who pushed Geordi backward, reached under the table, brought out a phaser rifle, and immediately fired at him. The blast struck Geordi in the chest and knocked him to the deck. Alarmed, Commander Hutchinson demanded to know what was going on. Meanwhile, the waiter had taken from under the table a second phaser rifle, which he now fired at Commander Hutchinson, killing him instantly. Unarmed, my senior staff was easily captured.

Back on the *Enterprise,* I was taken to main engineering. My presence came as a surprise to the technicians' leader, Kelsey. She wanted to know who I was. Sensing that it was unwise to reveal my true identity, I told her that I was "Mott," the ship's barber, that I wanted to go riding, had gone to get my saddle, and when I arrived at the transporter room found that primary power had been shut off. She told me "all right" and to "just shut up!" When Kiros reported that she hadn't found any signs of Devor, Kelsey ordered another technician to guard me and sent Kiros to search for him.

Sitting on the deck with one of the technicians guarding me, I overheard the other technicians talking about the field diverters they had installed in main engineering to protect them from the baryon sweep. Despite taking this precaution for their own safety, Kelsey said she was more concerned about protecting a storage unit—she wanted the trilithium resin in it before the baryon sweep hit main engineering. I then realized exactly what they were doing. They were draining trilithium resin from the *Enterprise*'s warp core. This substance is a highly volatile toxic waste produced by warp engines; it is of no useful purpose other than making very powerful weapons. Surely, I thought to myself, these people are terrorists!

Meanwhile, back on Arkaria Base, Counselor Troi sensed that Orton was agitated and nervous—as if something had gone wrong. If this was the case, Orton wasn't letting it be known. After capturing them, he had said nothing to my staff. Deducing that Geordi's discovery of the phaser rifles had upset the timetable for whatever Orton's plan had been, Data believed that the station administrator had no contingency plan for the situation, which was to my staff's advantage.

As Dr. Crusher attended to Geordi's wounds, Data suggested that it might be possible to modify the optical transducer in Geordi's VISOR so that it would generate a hypersonic pulse. Beverly observed that such a pulse would overload the audio receptors of everyone in the room and cause their immediate unconsciousness. However, as Data was an android, he would be unaffected. With everyone else unconscious, Data could take charge of the situation.

Agreeing to Data's plan, Will asked Beverly to make the modifications to Geordi's VISOR by herself, as if she were simply continuing to attend to his wounds. This would prevent Orton from becoming suspicious.

Back on the *Enterprise,* I watched as the technicians began to drain trilithium resin from the warp core. Knowing that it was my urgent duty to stop them.

The technicians hadn't expected me, the ship's barber, to be armed. Perhaps this is why they had failed to search me. Thanks to this lack of precaution, I still had Devor's communicator and laser torch.

As I sat on the deck with my back to the wall, I noticed a heat sensor directly behind me. My guard was paying more attention to his comrades than he was to me. Taking advantage of the situation, I discharged a blast from the torch into the sensor. The charge immediately caused the sensor to set off the main engineering compartment's fire extinguishers. Simultaneously, the compartment filled with fire-retardant gas and the fire wall began to close. The technicians were startled and confused! I jumped up and knocked my guard to the deck. Then I used the laser torch to destroy a field diverter. Now these terrorists wouldn't be protected from the baryon sweep, though neither would I.

50

I ran out of the main engineering compartment just before its fire door closed; my guard was close behind. Once in the corridor, I ran to a Jefferies tube, opened the hatch, and crawled inside. Crawling along the tunnel as fast as I could, I came to a hatch door. As I opened it, I saw the baryon sweep coming toward me. With the technician closing in on me from the other end of the tube, I had to act quickly. I took off my jacket and left it in front of the hatch. Then I made my way down another crawl space and out of the tube. The technician paused to inspect my jacket and couldn't see what was just beyond the closed hatch. I knew Worf kept hand-operated Klingon weapons in his quarters. They would be unaffected by the baryon sweep. As I made my way toward Worf's quarters, I heard the technician cry out in anguish as the baryon radiation beam swept through him.

Over the communicator I had taken from Devor, I heard Kelsey inform Kiros that they had discovered I was a Starfleet officer. Suspecting that I had killed Satler and maybe Devor, they knew that I had destroyed a field diverter in main engineering. Kelsey went on to tell Kiros that they were moving to Ten-Forward, as it was the last area of the ship that would be swept by the baryon beam—they were taking the trilithium resin with them.

On hearing her plans, I picked up the communicator and told Kelsey not to act foolishly: "Moving trilithium resin requires special equipment. You can't just improvise something."

Kelsey responded by telling me that if I was so concerned I shouldn't have destroyed the field diverter. I should just stay out of their way before I set off an explosion that would destroy the *Enterprise* and me.

I told Kelsey that I would rather destroy the ship than allow the trilithium resin to fall into the hands of terrorists. Coyly denying that she was a terrorist, Kelsey went on to inform me that they had been planning this action for a long time.

Knowing that there were few direct routes to Ten-Forward, I went to a shaft that I expected the technicians-cum-terrorists would use as they made their way to the lounge. Using the laser torch, I sheared enough successive ladder rungs to prevent them from accessing Ten-Forward through that particular passageway. Returning to Worf's quarters, I procured a crossbow and dipped a few arrows in a light tar laced with a sedative.

As I continued preparing a few surprises for the technicians, Kelsey signaled me over her communicator and informed me that they had discovered my sabotage of the ladder rungs in the shaft. Kelsey went on to say that my actions hadn't been very clever; if I really wanted to stop them, I should have attacked them directly. As it was, they would just have to find another way to Ten-Forward.

Kelsey went on to say that I should be trying to find a way off the *Enterprise*. I told her that I planned to leave the same way she was—on her ship. Admitting that she had arranged for her group to escape by way of a spaceship, Kelsey said it was a very small ship—there wasn't enough room for both of us. I told her that I was sorry to hear that—I would be sure to send her my regrets.

Out in the corridor, I lay in wait for the rebels. When one came walking toward me, I shot him with the crossbow. As I was taking a weapon out of the fallen technician's hand, Kiros suddenly appeared and took me captive. She reported my capture to Kelsey, and was given instructions on where to bring me.

Back on Arkaria Base, a perimeter warning sounded. It was a signal from the Remmler Array indicating the arrival of a small spacecraft. On hearing the signal, Orton went to the computer panel and lowered the base's defensive shields, which allowed the spacecraft to enter the area safely.

Although he was still a prisoner on the Starbase and unaware of what was taking place aboard the *Enterprise,* Commander Riker understood that whatever Orton was up to had to be stopped. Will whispered to Data that once the hypersonic burst had rendered everyone else unconscious, he should go to the computer panel and find a way to stop the approaching ship. Across the room, Beverly completed the modifications to Geordi's VISOR and activated the hypersonic burst. In an instant, everyone in the room—except Data—fell unconscious.

Back on the *Enterprise,* we were making our way to Ten-Forward. As we walked, I suggested to Kelsey that perhaps we could work out a deal. She responded to my suggestion by saying, "You're the only one who needs a deal, Mott!"

Now desperate to prevent the trilithium resin from falling into the wrong hands, I revealed my true identity and offered myself as her hostage in exchange for leaving the trilithium resin on the *Enterprise.* Kelsey told me that she wasn't a terrorist nor did she have a political agenda. But, she said, she knew some people who did. These people were very interested in the trilithium resin. As the theft was motivated entirely by profit, Kelsey said she would rather think of it as an act of commerce.

Arriving at Ten-Forward, I was first to enter the lounge and carefully stepped over the lines of explosive powders that I had earlier placed on the deck. Kiros didn't see the trap and stepped on the powder, which immediately ignited and sent a small flame into the air. The blast knocked both of the technicians to the deck. Kiros was rendered unconscious, and Kelsey was shaken just enough to let go of the canister containing the trilithium resin, which went rolling across the deck. Just as I lunged for one of their weapons that had fallen to the deck during the explosion, Kelsey attacked me. As we struggled, the baryon sweep began making its way through Ten-Forward. We fought for a few moments more before Kelsey picked up a weapon. Holding me at bay, she beamed off the *Enterprise* and onto the small ship that had come for her.

Time was running out for me. Now, only seconds remained before I would fall victim to the baryon sweep. Picking up one of the technicians' communicators, I hailed Arkaria Base and ordered them to deactivate the baryon sweep. There was no response to my signal. My death was now almost certain. While moving to the far front of Ten-Forward, I repeated my order to Arkaria Base. Then, just as the baryon sweep was about to destroy me, it suddenly stopped.

I was exhausted, but greatly relieved to hear Data calling to see if I was all right. I reported that I was. Data reported that an unidentified scout ship had just beamed off the *Enterprise.* "Do you know anything about it?"

Truthfully, I didn't know much about who, other than Kelsey, was on the ship. But during my fight with Kelsey, I had removed the safety pin from the canister containing the trilithium resin, which explains why my answer to Data's inquiry was simply "I know they won't get very far."

Turning to look out a window, I saw the scout ship explode. Fortunately, the trilithium resin wouldn't be used to make weapons for terrorists.

After the crew transported back to the *Enterprise,* Beverly ordered me to sickbay. However, besides my wounds, there was another urgent matter that needed attention—my saddle was missing! After an extensive search of our ship, Mr. Worf brought my saddle into sickbay. It had been found in a maintenance locker.

To be sure, saddles are not standard equipment aboard a starship. Just the same, while the *Enterprise* was docked at the Remmler Array, my saddle came in rather handy . . . I only wish that I could have used it on a horse.

Captain's personal journal: Observations on "Urgency." Stardate 46691.9. En route to the Borgolis Nebula.

An officer is constantly faced with situations that require his immediate attention. However, an officer should never act in too much haste, whether evacuating a starship or preventing its destruction. Situations also arise that require an officer to reorder his priorities, as was my experience at the Remmler Array. I assure you that I would have rather gone horseback riding than deal with criminal technicians attempting to steal a very dangerous substance from my ship.

However, one must forgo planned activities when matters of higher priority or crisis present themselves. Fortunately, I was ultimately able to prevent the theft of the trilithium resin even though it appeared that the action would cost me my life.

I must say that my senior staff acted quickly and properly when they became aware of problems at Arkaria Base. Despite the unfortunate death of Commander Hutchinson, my key officers acted with a sense of urgency that enabled them to regain control of the base. I cannot help but feel that had they hesitated to act, Data would not have been able to shut down the baryon sweep and save my life.

Moreover, as this event clearly illustrates, there are times when members of the crew can take urgent, independent action that adds to the collective resolution of a problem. I assure you that it is a pleasure to serve with officers I can trust to take action when such circumstances arise.

Captain's personal Journal: Lessons on "Urgency." Stardate 46697.2. Departing Bersallis III.

I think you will find that our experience while docked at the Remmler Array contains many important lessons dealing with urgency. Indeed, as a sense of urgency is a remarkable quality, I offer the following lessons for your consideration.

- Urgency should not be construed as haste, but as purposeful action. Such action should be deliberate and executed with patience. Deliberation is not delay, but consideration of options. Patience is not excess indulgence, but diligence. Indeed, the officer who acts with a sense of urgency is one who selects the best option to maximize opportunity at the most opportune time.
- Clearly, an officer who has a sense of urgency is one of intelligence. He knows what his mission is and the purpose for it. His energy is not blind, nor fitful, nor easily daunted.
- I am convinced that an officer who has a sense of urgency learns to master his circumstances and not to be mastered by them. Indeed, circum-

stances rarely prevent an officer who acts with a sense of urgency from succeeding at his mission.

- It is my experience that the most accomplished Starfleet officers are ones who have a sense of urgency in the performance of their duties and expect no less from their crew.

- In space, it is rarely better to act quickly and err than to tarry until the time of action has past, as the time of action for any one thing is rarely absolute and many errors are fatal.

- It is imperative to understand that in many difficult missions, a moment arises when a decision must be made if the mission is to succeed. Indeed, sensing when this moment has arrived is often more difficult than the decision itself.

- Acting with a sense of urgency brings ease as well as strength. Frequently, what we do with proper deliberation and patience is often done with less exertion and greater effectiveness.

- To be sure, some missions have limited time parameters, but virtually all missions have time enough to be successfully completed if a crew applies itself well.

- Acting with a sense of urgency, a crew first understands what is to be done, and then applies itself by doing what must be done until it achieves the best results of which it is capable.

And in closing,

- How much an officer accomplishes during his career in the Starfleet depends on his ability, opportunity, and application. The first two factors are largely fixed but can be modified. The third factor is largely in an officer's control. Indeed, he may determine the amount of application he will join with his ability and opportunity. Moreover, the results of his application are how his accomplishments are measured.

I am quite sure that each of you will meet with challenging missions during your career in Starfleet. Most certainly, some of these missions may be extraordinarily difficult to achieve. However, if you engage each mission . . . every duty . . . with a sense of urgency you will attain many marvelous accomplishments even under trying circumstances. Make it so.

III

Initiative

"Permission Granted"

Superintendent's foreword to "Initiative." *In the twenty-fourth century, the galaxy is plagued with predators and vagabonds eager to live off the profit from the fortunes of others, rather than to earn their own way by honest effort. Such people disgrace their own existence and rob value from others. It is also an era in which, despite having the most favorable incentives constantly before them, some people are quite satisfied to drift on the current of vacillation and casual exertion that yields nothing of consequence for themselves or the common good. These idlers hold no regard for their personal honor and add no value to their society.*

It is because of these opportunists, drifters, and freeloaders that the progress of all intergalactic life-forms rests firmly on those willing to fulfill the full measure of their existence by journeying along the valleys and over the hills of persistent and wearisome effort—people who honor their own existence and add great value to their societies.

This is also an era when the Federation has need of men and women with ambition—people who use their knowledge, imagination, abilities, and resources in a way that provides for the common good. For this reason, there is abundant room in the higher and more responsible positions in Starfleet for those who take initiative with or without being in the presence of their commanding officer.

Under the command of Captain Jean-Luc Picard, the Enterprise-D *maintained an environment where personal initiative was enculturated into young members of the crew, as it was expected of everyone. It followed then that for whatever purpose, when any of the* Enterprise's *crew asked for advance approval of even risky but well-reasoned and rightly intended action, their captain predictably responded with two words: "Permission granted."*

Admiral Andrea Brand
Superintendent, Starfleet Academy

Captain's personal journal: Stardate 46127.6. Enroute to Starbase 55.

Despite the sophistication of the *Enterprise*'s sensors and the competency and experience of my crew, there are times when we are unable to detect perils before us. Quite frankly, deep-space exploration is often met with danger and surprise, and mission success hinges on whether or not the crew will take the initiative to perform their duties in spite of the risks involved.

* * *

Shortly after assisting Lumerian ambassador Ves Alkar and his negotiators to secure a new Rekag-Seronia peace accord, which ended a conflict that was threatening Federation shipping routes, our sensors picked up a Federation distress signal. Commander Data determined the signal to be that of the *U.S.S. Jenolen,* a Federation transport reported missing in this sector seventy-five years ago. On coming out of warp speed, we had just changed course to lock on to and track the signal when the *Enterprise* was violently jolted by the force of her entry into an undetected, but massive, gravitational field.

As our charts listed no stars, planets, or other stellar bodies for this sector, we were curious as to the nature of this gravitational force. While Data attempted to localize the source of the gravitational field, an enormous sphere suddenly appeared on the main viewscreen. After further investigation, Data reported that the sphere's enormous mass had caused gravimetric interference with our sensors and prevented them from detecting it before we were virtually upon it.

We were both surprised and amazed at the sight of this object. I asked Mr. Data if he thought it could be a Dyson Sphere. He concluded that the object seemed to meet the general parameters of Dyson's theory. According to Professor Freeman Dyson, a twentieth-century physicist, an enormous hollow sphere could be constructed around a star, thereby harnessing all of its radiant energy. As such, the sphere would afford any population living inside its surface with virtually inexhaustible sources of power. Until this very moment, there had never been any known confirmation of Dyson's theory.

Commander Riker wondered if there could still be people living inside. Data responded to his question. He said there was a possibility that a very great number of people could be living inside this colossal structure.

While Mr. Riker, Data, and I speculated further about the sphere, Lieutenant Worf located the source of the distress signal. It was coming from a point in the Dyson Sphere's northern hemisphere. I immediately directed that the *Enterprise* be placed into synchronous orbit above that position. Soon after, Data located the *Jenolen,* which had impacted on the surface of the sphere. No life signs could be detected; however, there were several small power emanations and life-support was still functioning on minimal levels. Mr. Riker immediately ordered Commander La Forge and Lieutenant Worf to join him on an away team to investigate the *Jenolen*'s wreckage and determine the reason why some of this ship's systems were still functioning after seventy-five years.

Once on board the *Jenolen,* Geordi informed Commander Riker that the transporter was still on-line, but operating in an odd configuration. It was being fed power from the auxiliary systems, its rematerialization subroutine had been intentionally disabled, the phase inducers were connected to the emitter array, the override was completely gone, and the pattern buffer was locked into a continuous diagnostic cycle. While none of this made any sense to either of them, Geordi found a pattern still to be existing within the transporter's buffer. Will asked him if someone could survive inside a transporter buffer for seventy-five years. Geordi told him that he didn't know, but there was a way to find out, and activated the rematerialization subroutine.

Much to their astonishment, a man rematerialized before them and thanked Will and Geordi for bringing him out of the transporter buffer, and then went to the console, where he attempted to rematerialize Franklin, a man who had entered the buffer with him. His efforts were without success; Franklin's pattern had degraded beyond recovery.

Commander Riker then introduced himself and Commander La Forge to the man, and informed him that they were from the *Starship Enterprise,* which the man mistakenly believed to be the *U.S.S. Enterprise*-A. The man said that he wouldn't be surprised if Captain Kirk himself had brought the ship out of mothballs and sent her to rescue him and the others aboard the *Jenolen.* He then introduced himself as Captain Montgomery Scott and asked how long he had been missing. At this point, Commander Riker introduced our security chief to him; Captain Scott was rather taken back to see a Klingon warrior in a Starfleet officer's uniform — the last he knew, the Klingons and the Federation had just made peace. Sensing Captain Scott's bewilderment, Mr. Riker remarked that perhaps there were some things they should talk about.

After they had transported back to the *Enterprise,* Captain Scott began commenting on design changes in the ship. Mr. Riker suggested that Captain Scott should proceed to sickbay and have Dr. Crusher take a look at him. As Geordi escorted Captain Scott to sickbay, Captain Scott explained that he was a passenger on the *Jenolen,* which was taking him to Norpin V to live out his retirement. The *Jenolen* had suffered warp engine failure—an overload in one of the plasma transfer conduits—and hit some gravimetric interference when she came upon the Dyson Sphere. Captain Scott and the crew of the *Jenolen* were no less amazed at this extraordinary engineering feat than we were. They began their standard survey of the object's surface and were just completing their initial orbital scan when their aft power coil suddenly exploded. Franklin and Captain Scott were the only ones to survive the crash. Captain Scott rearrayed the *Jenolen*'s transporter in order for him and Franklin to survive while waiting their rescue.

Dr. Crusher found that Captain Scott had a hairline fracture of his left humerus as well as various bumps and bruises. Otherwise, he was in fine condition for a 147-year-old man. Pleasantly surprised to have such a distinguished Starfleet officer from an earlier generation on board my ship, I proceeded to sickbay and introduced myself to him. Dispensing with formalities, Captain Scott told me to call him "Scotty." I informed Scotty that I would thoroughly enjoy hearing him discuss his career and events of his time. However, for the time being, my presence was required on the bridge as we needed to immediately begin a spectrograph analysis of the Dyson Sphere's surface. As could be predicted of such a venerable engineer, Scotty wanted to assist with our analysis. But for the moment, Dr. Crusher ordered him to get some rest.

Notwithstanding, Scotty soon made his way to engineering and attempted to help, but Commander La Forge considered Scotty's presence to be a hindrance. Scotty soon became frustrated when his efforts to assist were neither welcomed nor needed and went to Ten-Forward. After Data helped him procure a bottle of Aldebaran whiskey, Scotty made his way to one of the holodecks. I later joined Captain Scott for a drink in the holodeck and we spoke about many things. Quite simply, I found Captain Scott—Scotty—to be a rather fascinating and delightful man.

Meanwhile, our sensors indicated the presence of a G-type star in the center of the sphere and that its interior to have a class-M atmosphere. While the Dyson Sphere was apparently capable of supporting life, there were no indications that it was still inhabited.

After returning to my ready room, I requested that Mr. La Forge meet with me. I told Geordi that it was my understanding that before the *Jenolen* crashed, her crew had conducted an extensive survey of the Dyson Sphere. Then I asked him if we had been able to access any of these records. Commander La Forge said that his staff had attempted to download the *Jenolen*'s computer memory core, but as it was heavily damaged in the crash, they had not yet been able to access the *Jenolen*'s records.

I suggested that perhaps Captain Scott could be useful in helping us access these survey records. Mr. La Forge agreed. He planned to have one of his staff beam back down to the *Jenolen* with Captain Scott. I suggested to Geordi that he accompany our guest. It was not an order, but a request, and one that I told Geordi he should feel perfectly comfortable to decline. Based on our conversation in the holodeck, I knew how important it was to Scotty that he be useful to us, and I wanted him to feel useful again. After hearing the reason for my request, Mr. La Forge agreed. Scotty and he were soon back on board the *Jenolen.*

Data informed Commander Riker that he had located what he thought to be a communications device on the sphere's surface. It was an antenna array emitting low-intensity subspace signals, located some four hundred thousand kilometers south of the *Enterprise*'s position. As Data could not open a communications channel with it from our present position, Commander Riker ordered the *Enterprise* to be placed in orbit above the array and called me to the bridge.

On our approach to the antenna array, we observed a large portal on the sphere's surface. Commander Riker believed the portal to be the door to a passageway that could lead us to the interior of the Dyson Sphere. Following standard Starfleet procedure, I had just asked Mr. Worf to open a channel to the communications array when some sort of tractor beam locked on to the *Enterprise.* All attempts to maneuver away from the portal and out of the tractor beam's grasp failed. We lost our main power, and our auxiliary power mysteriously dropped to twenty percent. Whatever had our ship in its clutches was pulling us directly into the sphere's interior.

Once the *Enterprise* was inside the sphere, the tractor beam released its hold. Mr. Data informed me that he was reading a great deal of surface instability on the star when we realized the inertial motion of the tractor beam was still propelling us forward, our impulse engines were still off-line, she couldn't stop our momentum—we were falling directly into the star!

Back on the *Jenolen,* Geordi and Scotty's efforts were still short of bringing the primary computer database back on-line. As they discussed the situation, Scotty recalled a device they used to have aboard his *Enterprise* that could possibly solve their dilemma. Geordi told Scotty that while he hadn't seen such a device in a long time, there was something back on our vessel that served the same purpose, and attempted to make contact with us. But as the *Enterprise* had left her position, Geordi's call went unanswered.

The *Enterprise* was three minutes from entering the star's photosphere. Her maneuvering thrusters had only thirty percent power, not enough to stop, but perhaps enough to turn into orbit and hold her distance from the star's photosphere. If we could not make it so, we would be destroyed!

Ordering the conn officer to reverse our thrusters, I was able to make a minor change to our flight path. However, the change in our course was insufficient, we were still headed into the star. Commander Riker then ordered engineering to divert all power from auxiliary relay systems to the maneuvering thrusters, which proved a wise initiative indeed. The rerouted power provided us with sufficient maneuverability to enter orbit some one hundred fifty thousand kilometers above the star's photosphere. Presumably, we could now operate safely, but little did any of us realize that another peril lay ahead.

Commander Riker went to see if he could get our main power back on-line. I asked Data to begin a scan of the sphere's interior for life-forms.

Meanwhile, Scotty suggested to Geordi that perhaps the *Enterprise* had crashed—just like the *Jenolen.* Geordi dismissed this idea as he couldn't pick up any background radiation that would have been present if we had gone down. Scotty quickly surmised another possibility—we could be inside the Dyson Sphere. Geordi responded with a "maybe," but wherever we were, he knew that they had to find us—words that set their initiative in motion.

Geordi suggested to Scotty that if they could get the *Jenolen*'s engines working again, they could track our impulse ion trail. Scotty protested such a challenge to be virtually impossible, and if they could restore the *Jenolen*'s engines, it would take longer than they had to find us. That said, and true to his legendary reputation, Scotty said there was no use crying about the situation. Before long, their newly formed sense of cooperation and corroboration was in full operation. And, as you might expect, with a few heroics and a great deal of ingenuity, they soon restored the *Jenolen*'s engines, and set about finding us.

Back on the *Enterprise,* Data reported that the sphere appeared to be abandoned. The star was extremely unstable, which explained why whoever built the Dyson Sphere had since departed. Data then said that he thought our attempts to communicate had triggered a series of automatic piloting beams designed to guide spacecraft inside the sphere. Just then, Worf informed me that his sensors were indicating a large magnetic disturbance on the star's surface. Data confirmed Worf's findings, adding that the star had entered a period of increased activity and our sensors were indicating that the solar flares would continue to grow. In three hours, our shields would no longer be sufficient to protect us—our situation was grim and worsening by the minute.

For their part, Geordi and Scotty had tracked the *Enterprise*'s ion trail right up to the portal through which we had entered the sphere. Scotty's analysis of the momentum distribution of our ion trail clearly indicated to him that the *Enterprise* had been forcibly drawn through the portal. Geordi commented that there appeared to be some sort of communications array near the portal. Scotty confirmed Geordi's findings and said that they had found hundreds of them during their initial survey seventy-five years ago. Geordi then asked Scotty if the *Jenolen* had tried communicating with the sphere. Scotty affirmed that they had. It was standard procedure at the time and they had tried it just before the *Jenolen* crashed. Aware that opening a communications channel with an unknown facility was still standard Starfleet procedure, Mr. La Forge quickly and accurately reasoned what had happened to the *Enterprise,* and he and Scotty soon arrived at a way to come to our aid. They would send out a signal that would cause the portal to open, but keep the *Jenolen* a sufficient distance from it to prevent her from being pulled inside. Scotty suggested that just as the portal was reclosing, they would maneuver the *Jenolen* between its doors and hold them open long enough for the *Enterprise* to escape. It was an imaginative but dangerous idea; the *Jenolen* would almost certainly be crushed. But the adventurous Captain Scott convinced Mr. La Forge that the *Jenolen*'s shields would protect them just long enough to get the job done. Obviously, the fact that they would be placing themselves in great danger was secondary to rescuing the *Enterprise* and its crew.

As we continued searching for a way out of our predicament, Commander La Forge maneuvered the *Jenolen* between the portal's doors—blocking them partially open—and hailed us. This time, his message was received and Geordi informed us of their position and that the *Jenolen*'s shields would not hold much longer. Geordi's message understood, I ordered a course toward the portal.

Aboard the *Jenolen* the situation began rapidly to deteriorate. The strain of blocking the portals doors open had taken a quick and heavy toll on the *Jenolen*'s engines and shields. As she rocked, Commander La Forge and Captain Scott attempted to maintain the *Jenolen*'s position. Mr. La Forge notified me that they were not going to be able to move the *Jenolen* out of our way. We would have to destroy them in order to clear the portal.

I understood what Geordi had said, but was not about

to destroy them. As such, I ordered the transporter operator to prepare to beam two from the *Jenolen* aboard as soon as we were within range. I then directed Mr. Worf to ready and arm two photon torpedoes. As soon as Data informed me that we were within transporter range, I ordered the transporter operator to energize and simultaneously ordered Mr. Worf to fire the torpedoes.

Let there be no mistake about it, this was a very risky move on my part—one that offered no margin of error. Regardless of the danger involved, I knew of no other option that would save Commander La Forge and Captain Scott while allowing our ship to escape. Much to everyone's good fortune, our combined tactics proved successful.

With Commander La Forge and Captain Scott safely back aboard the *Enterprise,* I informed Starfleet command of our discovery. They immediately dispatched two science vessels to study the Dyson Sphere. That done, the *Enterprise* was once again under way.

Captain's personal journal: Observations on "Initiative." Stardate 46152.9. En route to the Amargosa Diaspora.

True enough, our discovery of the Dyson Sphere was one of chance. However the rescue of Captain Montgomery Scott was an act of Will and Geordi's initiative. Indeed, the exploration of space involves both random and intentional discoveries. Perhaps this explains why the exploration of space is such a continually dangerous yet invigorating venture. On the *Jenolen* Will and Geordi neither asked for permission nor hesitated to act when there was a possibility that someone was still alive within the *Jenolen*'s transporter buffer. Indeed, Captain Scott was rescued because these two fine officers saw a reason to act and took the initiative to do so.

As our recent experience reveals, accidental discoveries can never be fully understood without someone taking the initiative to uncover what mysteries and wonders they may contain, despite the dangers involved. To be sure, we have yet to solve the mystery of who built the Dyson Sphere or just how they accomplished this marvelous engineering feat. Nonetheless, we do understand why they built it and why they later abandoned it.

Because he had been suspended in the *Jenolen*'s transporter buffer for seventy-five years, Captain Scott was not fully qualified to perform all engineering functions on a Galaxy-class starship. Nevertheless, he had not lost his ambition to make a difference, and what a difference he made in our rescue from the Dyson Sphere.

Quite understandably, Geordi was preoccupied with his duties related to our discovery of the Dyson Sphere and the *Jenolen*. Therefore, he could not accommodate many of Captain Scott's questions, nor could he perceive any way that the legendary engineer could assist him with his duties. Just the same, when presented with a problem that he could not solve alone, Geordi was not hesitant to combine his knowledge and experience with Scotty's in order to unite their efforts, which led to our rescue. It is also important to bear in mind that these two extraordinary engineers took the initiative to solve a problem of unknown parameters, even at great risk to their own safety. Perhaps this is one of the most important lessons one can learn about the kind of initiative that makes a difference in the progress of any organization.

I cannot fail to mention the initiative that the crew of the *Enterprise* showed in making well-reasoned attempts to escape what appeared to be our certain destruction inside the Dyson Sphere. But despite their competence and initiative, my crew could not fully effect our escape. Fortunately, they never gave up trying and were able to sustain our safety until Geordi and Scotty came to our rescue. Sure enough, however, our own initiative resulted in rescuing Geordi and Scotty from their own destruction. This is another important lesson in initiative. Despite your competence and ambition to use it, there are times when, without combining your efforts with those of others, you cannot succeed at your mission. And certainly there are those occasions when all competence, ambition, tenacity, and persistence cannot overcome conditions that are beyond your control and are ones sufficient to result in your failure. However, one must always proceed on the basis that one's efforts will be rewarded, lest one become too discouraged to try to use knowledge and experience to solve problems and turn the course of events in one's favor.

Captain's personal Journal: Lessons on "Initiative." Stardate 46193.2. Departing the Amargosa Diaspora.

Initiative is an important quality that every officer must learn how to use to perform routine duties and to work through crisis situations. It is also a quality that an officer should develop and reinforce among his crew. For these reasons, I offer the following lessons on initiative for your consideration.

- In deep space, conditions rarely favor even the most experienced officer or crew. Therefore, most mission success depends upon those who are willing to work through obstacles with tenacious and persistent effort.
- An officer is not so much the product of his time as time becomes what an officer makes of it.
- An officer or crewman's initiative should be neither blind, fitful, nor easily distracted, and can only be taken when he fully understands his commander's intentions or when he knows what is expected of him under the circumstances.
- There is nothing more limiting of one's potential than too much fear of the unknown.
- I do not hold the conviction that fate falls on one despite his action or inaction. Rather, I believe one who fails to act places altogether too much faith in his fate.

- As a tendency toward hesitation can quickly become a habit, a crew member who habitually hesitates to act on his knowledge and experience is perhaps of less value to others than another who lacks the knowledge and experience to initiate action.
- Personal initiative is not a quality people have in equal volume. Therefore, an officer must learn to urge, to suggest, and occasionally to restrain others.
- Indeed, one's initiative is a direct expression of one's ambition, which ambition should always be expressed in action that provides for the common good.
- While there are times when one is granted considerable freedom to act, such freedom does not grant one impunity from violating laws or the basic rights of others.
- Quite simply, the great difference between insignificant and exceptional achievement is often a matter of the enthusiasm and determination by which one carries out one's duties.
- An officer who feels he must control every action taken by his crew destroys their will to take initiative when he is not present.

And by way of conclusion,

- As we have come to understand, the success of difficult missions, as well as the progress of our people, is often due to those who acted when action was required, and those who acted when others saw no reason to take action.

During my command of the *Enterprise,* I have taken every opportunity to encourage and reward personal initiative in the crew. Quite frankly, it has often been the crew's initiative that has made a difference in the success and safety of our missions. I would advise you to do the same. Also, when you are asked for approval of an action, you should find every reason to respond with "Permission granted." Make it so.

IV

Competence

"The Force Multiplier"

Superintendent's foreword to "Competence." *Airless and cold, its innumerable celestial bodies set in perpetual motion, space is without beginning or end. Governed by the power of its own forces, space has no respect for person or government. It neither harbors ill will for travelers seeking selfish gain nor grants special favor to those in pursuit of a noble cause. It is dangerous for even the prepared, yet unforgiving of the inept.*

While humanoids and other life-forms have traveled into the far reaches of interstellar space for thousands of millennia, only four centuries have past since the first manned spacecraft orbited Earth. Unlike primitive civilizations where competitive advantage favored whoever could amass the largest force, this is an age in which brain rules over brawn. To be certain, the productive applications of technology yield far greater results than the most arduous labors of human effort in the production of goods, search for knowledge, discovery of the unknown, or mortal combat.

The twenty-fourth century is also an era in which all advanced societies possess some technology having a degree of advantage over that held by other civilizations or alliances. But, as there is abundant and highly sophisticated technology to be found among all advanced species, technology is no longer the great force multiplier that it once was.

It is also true that just as leaders have never been more effective than the people around them, even if equipped with sophisticated technology, the poorly trained and ineffectively led can never perform at their best. Consequently, competence has now replaced technology as the force multiplier in this era of interstellar travel.

Admiral Andrea Brand
Superintendent, Starfleet Academy

Captain's personal journal: Stardate 47573.2. Departing the Argaya System.

I have every confidence that the greatest asset the Federation has is neither its starships, weapons, science labs, communication systems, nor its starbases, but the competence of the men and women who serve in Starfleet Command. For over two hundred years, the Federation has remained strong because of the competence of the people who serve in its Starfleet. It is with a profound sense of both sorrow and admiration that I have chosen the events of recent days to illustrate this conviction.

* * *

While the *Enterprise* was on course for a rendezvous with the *U.S.S. Clement,* Mr. Riker and other members of my senior staff were preparing crew evaluations and deciding which one of our junior officers should be promoted to an important position in Operations. Commander Riker was also conducting battle drills. Individual performance during these drills would be considered as part of each person's evaluation. I assure you that no one was taking these evaluations lightly.

In Ten-Forward, Commander Riker remarked to Counselor Troi that while Ensign Lavelle was the most obvious candidate for the Operations job, he was also considering Ensign Sito. Mr. Riker's comments were overheard by a barman who relayed the conversation to Ensigns Lavelle and Sito. This heightened Mr. Lavelle's concern over his future and caused Ensign Sito new worries. Why was she being considered for a position in Ops? After all, for the past seven months she had been a security officer on the *Enterprise.* Until now, she had considered her career path to be in Tactical.

Our mission to rendezvous with the *Clement* was interrupted when I received a coded message from Starfleet containing secret orders—orders so secret that the only aspect of this new mission I could reveal on the bridge was that the *Enterprise* was to set a new course and proceed at maximum warp to the Argaya System.

It is my customary practice to keep the entire crew well informed about the nature of all our missions.

However, this mission was extraordinarily dangerous and lives were at risk. For security reasons, I could only share the precise nature of this mission on a strict need-to-know basis.

Frankly, it was to our good fortune that we were coincidentally preparing crew evaluations as they provided some useful distraction from mission-related activities taking place aboard the *Enterprise*. Although I must admit that when legitimate questions about our mission couldn't be answered, it created some awkward moments for both parties to the conversation. As expected, this circumstance also gave rise to some imaginative suspicions and a few innocuous rumors among the crew. Despite these unusual conditions, we had to proceed with the mission on that basis.

During transit to the Argaya System, the senior staff continued their crew evaluations, while several of the crew did things they hoped would either impress their commanding officer or allow them to become better acquainted with another of my senior staff. Indeed, it is normal for talented people to desire to have their talents made known. This is especially true during crew evaluations or when an important job is in the offing.

Ensign Taurik, a young engineering officer who took his work seriously, attempted to involve Commander La Forge with a simulation that tested a new warp-field configuration.

Nurse Ogawa was another one of the crew being evaluated, but she was less concerned about the results of her evaluation than about doing her job well and keeping Dr. Crusher informed on patient conditions. I found this to be rather refreshing.

Ensign Sito was excited when Commander Riker asked her to fill in at Ops while I briefed Data and others about our new mission. She later discussed her experience with her commanding officer, Lieutenant Worf, in Ten-Forward. After listening to her retell this experience, Mr. Worf told his young protégé that Ops was a very different challenge from Tactical. Ensign Sito agreed and said that was why she could not figure out why she was being considered for the Ops job—she was a Security officer. The answer to her question came from Mr. Worf—he had recommended her.

Ensigns Lavelle and Taurik happened to be sitting across the lounge from Worf and Ensign Sito. Mr. Lavelle wondered aloud to his friends if perhaps Mr. Worf was giving Ensign Sito pointers on how to land the Ops position. Ensign Taurik asked his friend if he had ever considered learning to lip-read; then Commander Riker entered Ten-Forward. As Mr. Riker walked toward the bar, the barman Ben shouted across the lounge, "Hi, Will!" Commander Riker continued his stride and answered Ben's familiar greeting with "Ben."

This casual familiarity took Ensign Lavelle by surprise. After all, Commander Riker was second-in-command of the *Enterprise*. Ben reminded Ensign Lavelle that Commander Riker was a civilian when he came to Ten-Forward and wanted to be treated like a civilian. Ensign Lavelle still had doubts that Mr. Riker was approachable about anything that didn't involve official duties.

After learning that Mr. Lavelle believed his commanding officer disliked him, Ben told the ensign that maybe he felt this way because he hadn't gotten to know Commander Riker. Armed with a little encouragement and some facts about Mr. Riker's background and interests, Mr. Lavelle mustered up the courage to walk over to the bar and attempted to engage his commander in casual conversation. Much to Ensign Lavelle's disappointment, however, his effort faltered, which only furthered his erroneous belief that Mr. Riker just didn't care for him.

On arrival at our designated position in the Argaya System, Worf reported that he detected no vessels in the vicinity. Data had just reported that we were less than five thousand kilometers from the Cardassian border when a sensor warning sounded. Worf informed us that sensors had detected a small object that appeared to be an escape pod. Mr. Riker believed this to be an indication that the person we were to rendezvous with had been forced to abandon his ship. The object was still fifty thousand kilometers inside Cardassian space, and I wondered aloud, "How the hell are we going to get it out of there?"

A few moments later, Data detected that the escape pod's life-support system was failing. We had to act immediately. Already precariously close to the Cardassian border, we moved closer to get within transporter range. Still, without crossing over into

Cardassian territory, it was necessary to boost the gain of the transporter's confinement beam by seven percent to beam the person in the escape pod aboard the *Enterprise.*

Ensign Taurik had helped Commander La Forge in boosting the energy of the confinement beam. He was about to attempt life-form identification when Geordi informed him, "No one told you to do that, Ensign. Let's just get him aboard safely." Unaccustomed to having his normal duties interfered with, Mr. Taurik found Geordi's abruptness curious.

In sickbay, Dr. Crusher was being assisted by Nurse Ogawa in making preparations to receive our guest. When Beverly was informed that her patient was on the way, she thanked Nurse Ogawa and told her that she would have to leave.

Both Geordi and Beverly's directives were unfamiliar ones. Under normal circumstances, initiative and collaboration are encouraged and rewarded aboard the *Enterprise.*

Departing sickbay, Nurse Ogawa was surprised to find Ensign Sito standing guard outside the door and asked her friend what she was doing there. Ensign Sito told her everything she knew: she was not to allow anyone but senior officers into the area. It was an unusual security measure, which caused them both to wonder just what was going on.

I had gone to sickbay to get a report on the condition of our guest. Satisfied that Dr. Crusher had matters well under control, I left. As I departed sickbay, I ordered

Ensign Sito to accompany me. After we entered the turbolift, I asked Ensign Sito if she was a certified pilot, and she confirmed that she was.

We went to my ready room, where I commented to Ensign Sito that I understood she had been recommended for the Ops position, and asked if she thought she was up to it. Ensign Sito felt she was. I told her that I was not so sure. I had concerns about her record—concerns that stemmed from a cover-up she participated in at Starfleet Academy.

Ensign Sito was one of several cadets involved in Nova Squadron's attempt to impress guests attending their graduation exercises by performing a Kolvoord Starburst—a maneuver prohibited because of its extreme risks. This foolish attempt at impressing others resulted in the death of one of the Nova Squadron's crew. It was a senseless death, one that the rest of the crew attempted to cover up by attributing it to other causes. Wesley Crusher had also been a member of Nova Squadron. Because the Board of Inquiry lacked any firm evidence to the contrary, it appeared that the members of Nova Squadron would be exonerated from any responsibility for the death of their classmate. However, they were not acquitted. After I discussed the matter and an officer's first duty with Wesley, he confessed the truth about this incident and punishments were handed out.

Ensign Sito tried to dismiss my concerns by reminding me that the incident had taken place over three years ago and that her record since then—I interrupted and said that it didn't matter how long ago it had taken place. "Would you do something like that again?"

She assured me that she would never jeopardize lives . . . by—I interrupted again and finished her sentence. "By participating in a daredevil stunt. I would certainly hope not!"

Although she confessed that she should have been truthful from the beginning, I reminded Ensign Sito that she hadn't, which told me that she was lacking in character.

Ensign Sito pleaded for my understanding. After the incident she had no friends at the Academy, no one to talk to, and she had to take her flight test with the instructor because no one else would be her partner. She went on to say that in many ways it would have been easier to have just walked away, but she didn't. She had stuck with it and believed that to say something about her character.

I told her that I was very sorry that she didn't enjoy her time at the Academy but as far as I was concerned she should have been expelled for what she did. Then I said, "Quite frankly, I don't know how you made it aboard this ship. You're dismissed."

What Ensign Sito didn't understand was that I was testing her mettle. Ordinarily, I refrain from being either rude or abrasive with a subordinate, even when giving one a reprimand.

Then, to carry out a deception that would later play an important role in our larger mission, I asked Geordi, assisted by Ensign Taurik, to damage one of our shuttlecraft, making it appear as if it had been hit with phaser fire while engaging evasive maneuvers. Security precautions precluded Mr. La Forge from telling Ensign Taurik why the phaser blasts to the shuttle's hull were necessary.

Meanwhile, Nurse Ogawa's assistance was required to synthesize some Cardassian blood for our mystery patient. Dr. Crusher informed her that she was not to discuss what she was about to see with anyone. This too, was an extraordinary directive. Quite simply, Nurse Ogawa was neither one to reveal medical information to unauthorized members of the crew nor one known to break confidences.

Later that evening, both the junior officers and my senior staff relaxed in separate poker games. While the junior officers speculated why we were so close to the Cardassian border and who was in the escape pod, the senior staff discussed other matters.

Will mentioned to Worf that he didn't think Ensign Sito was the right one for the Ops job. Worf disagreed and told Commander Riker that it was his decision, but if he would give Ensign Sito a chance, she would prove herself. Will said that he would; besides, he still wasn't sure about Lavelle because he was too eager to please and made too many attempts to ingratiate himself with his commander. Counselor Troi didn't think such behavior unusual for someone who was trying to get a promotion. She went on to remind Will that perhaps he had done the same by playing poker with his senior officers while serving on the *Potemkin*. Then she added, "Your senior officers might have thought that you were trying to ingratiate yourself. I guess it's lucky that they realized you were young and inexperienced and decided not to hold it against you."

Deanna's observation was sufficient to cause Will to admit that perhaps he had been a little too hard on Ensign Lavelle.

Back at the junior officers' poker game, Ensign Sito discussed our early meeting. As I expected she would, Ensign Sito had taken our encounter hard and thought me to be unfair. And, to be sure about it, none of her friends thought it fair that I would block her promotion to Ops over something that had happened in the past.

Someone also suggested to Ensign Lavelle that perhaps he shouldn't try so hard to please Commander Riker. After all, if Mr. Riker had so much dislike for him, he wouldn't be a candidate for the Ops job. Lavelle agreed and added that maybe he was trying to convince himself that Commander Riker didn't like him just in case he didn't get the job—he'd have an excuse.

Ensign Taurik told his companions that he found it curious that Commander La Forge seemed annoyed that a junior officer's technique for warp-field configuration was actually more efficient than the *Enterprise*'s present configuration. A short time later, Commander La Forge entered the room and invited Ensign Taurik to join him in some experiments in engineering—an invitation Mr. Taurik was pleased to accept. Make no mistake about it, Geordi has never been one to hold back a junior officer's ideas, nor is he one to dismiss a subordinate's suggestions.

The next morning, Worf completed his basic martial-arts class for the day and asked Ensign Sito to remain behind. He informed her that he also taught an advanced class and thought she might be ready to participate, but first she would have to pass the *Gik'tal,* an ancient Klingon ritual that tests knowledge of basic martial-arts forms. Worf went on to tell her that there was no practice for the test—being unannounced was part of the ritual. Ensign Sito agreed to take the test.

Worf blindfolded his student and commanded her to defend herself. Of course, she couldn't. After being thrown several times, Ensign Sito took off the blindfold and said she refused to continue. "It's not a fair test."

Mr. Worf congratulated his student. She had passed the test. The test was all about courage, and it took courage to say that the test was unfair. As she understood the Klingon language, Ensign Sito knew *Gik'tal* to mean until the death. She also correctly perceived that there was no such test.

Worf admitted that the test had been contrived. Then he said, "But maybe the next time you are judged unfairly, it will not take so many bruises for you to protest."

What she hadn't realized before, she now understood: Mr. Worf was using this artificial ritual to teach her a great lesson about life—one she immediately put to use.

After changing into her duty uniform, Ensign Sito

came to visit me in my ready room. She boldly informed me that all she had ever wanted was to make a career for herself in Starfleet. There was nothing she could now do about past mistakes. She was willing to work hard to try to earn the respect of the people with whom she now served. If I wouldn't give her that chance, she wanted to be transferred to another ship!

Such bold courage has always impressed me. Nevertheless, I told Ensign Sito that if she was looking for a more lenient commander, I didn't think she would find one. Ensign Sito then asked my permission to speak freely. Of course, I granted her request.

Ensign Sito told me that if I hadn't wanted her to serve aboard the *Enterprise,* I should have said so when she was assigned to it. Furthermore, it was not my place to punish her for errors made while at the Academy, and that she should be judged for her record under my command.

Indeed, I was impressed and informed the young ensign that I *would* judge her by her present record. Moreover, I told her that it took courage to face me after what I had said in our previous meeting, the purpose of which I could now reveal. My purpose had not been to assess her qualifications for the Ops position. I had been harsh with her because I wanted to assess her for a very important mission, "a mission that . . . could put you in a situation that would be far more unnerving than a dressing-down by your commanding officer."

Ensign Sito wanted to know what the mission was. Instead of saying more at the time, I invited her to join the senior officers and me in the observation lounge at 0900 hours to discuss it. As she left my ready room, I felt obliged to inform Ensign Sito that I was the one who had chosen her to serve aboard the *Enterprise*—I had wanted to make certain that she was given a fair chance to redeem herself. And indeed she had.

Promptly at 0900 hours, Ensign Sito joined us in the observation lounge. Being Bajoran, Ensign Sito was surprised to see a Cardassian in our midst. Obviously she recalled the atrocities the Cardassians were responsible for inflicting upon her homeworld.

I introduced Joret Dal. He was a member of the Cardassian military and a Federation operative. He had risked his life to bring us vital information about Cardassian strategic intentions—information that could very well enhance the security of Bajor and other planets in the sector. Our mission was to protect Joret Dal's identity as a spy and to return him safely to Cardassian space.

It would be dangerous for Joret Dal to cross the heavily guarded Cardassian border without a cover story, so we were providing him with one. We would provide Joret Dal with the shuttlecraft that Geordi and Ensign Taurik had intentionally damaged. Joret Dal would profess to be a bounty hunter and claim to have stolen a Federation shuttle, escaping our space after coming under phaser fire. Joret Dal would be returning to Cardassian space with Ensign Sito, a Bajoran terrorist, as his prisoner. This cover story, along with a bribe, would gain Joret Dal safe passage. Once safely across the border, Ensign Sito would use the shuttle's escape pod to return to Federation space. We would be waiting for her return.

It was my duty to ensure that Ensign Sito understood this would be an extraordinarily dangerous mission—one I would not order her to take part in. Despite my concerns for her safety, she accepted without hesitation by saying, "Then, I volunteer, sir."

Satisfied that Ensign Sito fully understood the risks she was taking—no one knows better than a Bajoran what Cardassians do with their prisoners—I directed her to sickbay. Dr. Crusher would make it appear as if Ensign Sito—disguised as a Bajoran terrorist—had been mistreated by her Cardassian captor. Nothing less would be expected. I also informed her that she must not discuss this mission with anyone. She acknowledged that she understood my order. As Ensign Sito departed for sickbay, Joret Dal remarked that he didn't realize she would be so young. A point well taken, but moot. Despite her youth, Ensign Sito was fully competent to carry out her assignment.

Ensign Sito shortly returned to the shuttlebay. Her disguise complete with clothing suited for a Bajoran terrorist, Ensign Sito approached Mr. Worf, her mentor and commanding officer. She told him that she really appreciated the fact that he had always had confidence in her capability.

Moments later, Joret Dal and Ensign Sito were on their way into Cardassian territory.

We proceeded to the coordinates in Federation space where Ensign Sito's escape pod was to rendezvous with the *Enterprise*. However, we had been in the area for over thirty hours, there had been no sign of her approach.

My concern over her safety grew by the hour. We conducted long-range scans for life signs, but none could be detected. Becoming impatient with the situation, Mr. Worf recommended that we prepare a probe and send it into Cardassian territory to look for his young protégé. Commander Riker reminded us that launching a probe into Cardassian space would be a treaty violation. Regardless, Ensign Sito was a member of my crew. As such, I was responsible for her safety. Therefore, despite the treaty, I instructed Mr. Worf to prepare a probe and launch it when ready.

Shortly after the probe was launched, Data informed me that sensors were detecting signs of debris some two hundred thousand kilometers inside Cardassian space. Data believed the debris could possibly be the remains of a Federation escape pod. It wasn't long after this discovery that we intercepted a Cardassian report stating that a Bajoran prisoner had escaped her captor. The prisoner was killed in an evacuation pod as she tried to leave Cardassian space.

Protecting Joret Dal's identity as a Federation operative remained a continuing responsibility. Therefore, although I still could not reveal the exact nature of her mission, as captain of the *Enterprise* it became my duty to report this sorrowful event to the entire crew.

From my ready room, I announced, "To all Starfleet personnel, this is the captain. It is my sad duty to inform you that a member of the crew, Ensign Sito

Jaxa, has been lost in the line of duty. She was the finest example of a Starfleet officer, and a young woman of remarkable courage and strength of character. Her loss will be deeply felt by all who knew her. Picard out."

I assure you, truer words I have never spoken.

Captain's personal journal: Observations on "Competence." Stardate 47609.5. Near Barkon IV.

Individual and crew competence is the great force multiplier that can make one Starship more capable than another. Competence is also what distinguishes one member of the crew from another when being considered for assignment or promotion. As competence can be viewed from several vantage points, it is always good to have crew evaluations discussed among those officers who ultimately determine the assignments and promotions of the individuals being evaluated. This is why my senior staff collaborates on crew evaluations, and I must say that this process has proven to be an effective means for placing competent people in responsible jobs.

During this mission, our junior officers displayed predictable concern over the outcome of their evaluations and future assignments. I assure you that my key officers were similarly concerned that their evaluations of the crew be fair and accurate reflections of job performance and potential for positions of greater responsibility. Indeed, while Ensign Lavelle was promoted to the Ops position, we were considering several options for giving Ensign Sito the opportunity to progress through the ranks of Starfleet at an accelerated pace—options that became moot when her life was taken at the hand of the Cardassians.

You must also recognize that competence has to be nurtured and developed. Indeed, even as reflected during this mission in the cases of Mr. Worf with Ensign Sito, Mr. La Forge with Ensign Taurik, Dr. Crusher with Nurse Ogawa, and Mr. Riker with Ensign Lavelle. It is also imperative that you understand that this nurturing and development can take many forms and come in many guises.

When our mission called for a member of the crew to undertake a very dangerous assignment, it became necessary to choose the most competent person for that particular job. As Ensign Sito was qualified as a pilot and proved that she had the strength of character this mission demanded, she was chosen for it. I have every confidence that her tragic death was caused by reasons beyond her control. Had she survived, Ensign Sito would have had a distinguished career in the Starfleet.

Captain's personal journal: Lessons on "Competence." Stardate 47611.3. En route to rendezvous with the **U.S.S. Lexington.**

As officers of the Starfleet, you will be expected to competently perform all aspects of your duties. You will also be held responsible for seeing that your subordinates competently perform their duties as well. To these ends, I offer you the following lessons on competence.

- No matter what knowledge one has acquired, it requires the illustration and confirmation of experience to become wisdom.
- An officer should broaden his knowledge with and through others. He should also correct and complete his experience through the experience of others.
- It is impossible to master any art or science at once. Instead, to excel at anything one must patiently wrestle with it until it gives up its secret.
- One officer equipped with technology and tools that he cannot competently use has little, if any, advantage over another who possesses inferior devices and instruments.
- Perhaps the danger that least threatens an officer's effectiveness is the danger of knowing too much. However, it is possible to become very learned and yet be unable to make one's learning of any use. For this reason, it is essential that an officer acquire knowledge that can be put to use in Starfleet.
- No one becomes competent by passive experience. If experience is to add to one's knowledge and skill, it must be reflected and reacted upon with conscious effort to learn what lessons it may contain.

- A portion of an officer's power comes with the position he holds. However, the greatest measure of his power comes by knowing his work.
- Within Starfleet, a higher value is placed on an officer with the full mental ability to adapt readily to varied demands and unusual situations, and who can meet emergencies with inventiveness, than is placed on an officer who has but mere imitative skill.
- One of the surest ways to instill competence among the crew is to help them overcome their miscalculations before errors become habits.

In conclusion,

- Self-confidence is a positive attribute of an officer, but not sufficient enough to ensure his effectiveness. To become effective, an officer must provide his crew with the instruction and experience that will enable them to succeed.

The Federation places a high priority on the competency of the men and women who serve in its Starfleet. Becoming a competent officer should be your top priority upon completion of your courses at the Academy. But bear in mind that one can never become too competent; there is always something more to learn, always someone with whom to share your learning and experiences, and always another whose knowledge and experiences can enhance your competence. Indeed, competence is a force multiplier. Make it so.

V

Communication

"Understood"

Superintendent's foreword to "Communication."
*In the twenty-fourth century, advances in technology
have led to the development of highly evolved data,
visual, and voice communications systems and devices. These systems and devices provide the means
for sending and receiving messages between people
far and near.*

*It is also true that encounters between the Federa-
tion and people of different species, cultures, ideolo-
gies, and languages are common in this era of
interstellar travel. As such, mutually understandable
communication is an indispensable part of everyday
life. For this reason, it became necessary for Federation scientists to develop even more elaborate communication technology.*

*The Universal Translator is a complex, high-speed
computer that analyzes the patterns of unknown*

forms of communication and derives a translation matrix, which permits comprehensible voice and data exchanges between the Federation and alien life-forms. Although the Universal Translator constantly updates its database, its effectiveness is sometimes limited by distortions that arise when the language concepts, vocabulary, or word usage being processed vary too far from the sample on which the translation matrix is based.

And so it is that despite the sophistication of the Federation's technology, the fundamental challenge of effective communication in the twenty-fourth century remains as it was in all preceding millennia: messages given must not only be received, they must also be understood. To be sure, this challenge cannot be met by communications technology alone.

Admiral Andrea Brand
Superintendent, Starfleet Academy

Captain's personal journal: Stardate 45068.1. Departing the El-Adrel System.

It is true that communication in space often involves both speaking and listening over highly sophisticated devices. However, I don't think that technology itself can make communication effective. A more thorough examination of communication reveals that it is never effective without understanding, which may explain why failed attempts at communication can often lead to dangerous situations. And as I recently learned, despite our advanced means of communication, there are times when the most effective method of communication is a face-to-face encounter.

* * *

Starfleet picked up a subspace signal coming from a Tamarian spacecraft located near the uninhabited El-Adrel System. While the message was indecipherable, it contained a standard mathematical progression taken by the Federation as an indication that the Tamarians were attempting to communicate with us.

During the past hundred years, the Federation had attempted to establish dialogue with the Tamarians on seven previous occasions. Also known as the "Children of Tama," an advanced race, the Federation found the Tamarians to be enigmatic. Quite simply, their language was so incomprehensible that even the Universal Translator had failed to develop a matrix capable of translating it. As a result, all previous attempts to establish communications with them had been unsuccessful. But as these attempts had also gone without incident, the Federation believed the Tamarians to be a peaceful, well-intentioned race, which explains why we also believed that our two very different cultures shared some common values.

As the Federation's flagship, Starfleet gave the *Enterprise* the mission to once again attempt to establish formal relations with the Tamarians. The Tamarian vessel was detected as being located near El-Adrel IV. For the past three weeks, the Tamarians had been steadily transmitting their signal toward Federation space.

Under way to El-Adrel IV, I discussed our mission with my senior staff. Worf suggested that the Tamarians might be a threat to the Federation's border. However, based on all previous contact with them,

Starfleet believed the Tamarians to be extending an open hand to us.

Experience has taught me that communication is often a matter of patience and imagination, and I told my staff, "I would like to believe that these [patience and imagination] are qualities that we have in sufficient measure." Indeed, I felt this lesson of my experience held the answer to how we could succeed where others had failed.

Coming into synchronous orbit with the Tamarian spacecraft, we opened a communications channel with them. On the viewscreen we were greeted by the Tamarian captain, who spoke in words and phrases that we could not understand, even with the aid of our Universal Translator. However, Counselor Troi sensed them to have nothing but good intentions. Attempting to decipher their language, Data observed that the Tamarian captain seemed to be stating the proper names of individuals and locations. Despite these observations, we still could not understand the Tamarian captain.

I rose from my command chair and walked closer to the viewscreen. Taking the initiative, I asked the Tamarian captain, "Captain, would you be prepared to consider the creation of a mutual nonaggression pact between our two peoples . . . possibly leading to a trade agreement and cultural interchange? Does this sound like a reasonable course of action to you?"

His response was puzzling. The Tamarian captain and others on his ship's bridge broke into laughter and continued to converse in words we could not understand. We then witnessed a conversation between the Tamarian captain and one who appeared to be his first officer, but we couldn't make out what they were saying. As they ended their discussion, the captain took a dagger from a sheath the other Tamarian wore across his chest. Reaching to his own chest sheath, the captain withdrew a second dagger. Now directly facing the viewscreen, the captain raised both daggers and said, "Darmok and Jalad at Tanagra."

Precisely at the moment he finished this incomprehensible phrase, the Tamarian captain energized—as did I. Without warning, the Tamarians had transported us to the planet's surface. The Tamarian ship simultaneously created a particle-scattering field on the planet's ionosphere—making it impossible for Chief O'Brien to transport me back to the *Enterprise*.

I found myself standing in a small meadow surrounded by thick brush and small trees, and was attempting to orient myself, when I heard a rustling noise and turned to see what or who was there. It was the Tamarian captain—daggers in hand. This time, however, the Tamarian raised them above his head, but said nothing—he just stood and stared at me.

As I was later to learn, Commander Riker attempted to contact me, but his efforts were to no avail. The Tamarian ship was projecting a particle-suspending beam into the upper atmosphere, which kept their particle-scattering field in place and disrupted communications between either the *Enterprise* or their ship and the planet's surface. However, the Tamarians had left sensor frequencies clear, allowing both the *Enter-*

prise and their ship to partially monitor what was happening on the planet. Thus, Mr. Worf detected what he thought to be a contest between two champions—the Tamarian captain and me. Worf's report alarmed Commander Riker, as he recalled that the Tamarian captain was armed.

Meanwhile, on El-Adrel IV, the Tamarian captain lowered his weapons. Then he walked toward me while repeating, "Darmok and Jalad." I took his actions as an indication that he wanted to fight with me. In response, I told the Tamarian that I neither knew who or what Darmok or Jalad were nor did I intend to fight. My words seemed mute. The Tamarian tossed one of the daggers on the ground before me and said, "Darmok and Jalad at Tanagra."

Cautiously, I picked up the dagger and tossed it back, saying to him, "Sorry, Captain."

Shaking his head in frustration, the Tamarian muttered, "Shaka . . . when the walls fell . . ." as he picked up the dagger. Putting the dagger in his chest sheath, the Tamarian turned and walked away.

Meanwhile, Commander Riker hailed the Tamarian vessel and ordered its first officer to release me. Otherwise, their actions could be interpreted as an act of war. Although neither party could understand the other's words, what Will saw over the viewscreen gave him concern. By his tone of voice and body language, the Tamarian first officer appeared to be communicating aggressive intentions. As such, Commander Riker ordered the communications channel closed and directed Worf to assemble a security team, take a shuttle down to the planet's surface, and bring the captain back.

Evening fell and the air began to chill. I attempted to light a fire, but my efforts failed. About twenty meters away, the Tamarian had already built his own small campfire, and I heard him laughingly say, "Shaka. When the walls fell."

Keeping our distance, we continued speaking to one another. Still, neither one of us could understand the other's words or intentions. Indeed, if I didn't freeze to death first, I suspected the Tamarian might attack me during the night. Just then, the Tamarian captain said, "Darmok of Kanza. Jalad of the Kituay."

I looked across the way at him and said, "Picard of the Federation."

The Tamarian didn't seem to understand me. So I added, "Of the *Starship Enterprise* . . . Of the planet Earth."

Despite my attempts to communicate, my words meant nothing to the Tamarian. And I heard him mutter, "Kadir beneath Mo Moteh . . ."

The Tamarian then began a strange ritual. He took some small ornamental metal objects from his uniform and began placing them around his position and making hand gestures toward the sky. Then, taking one of the daggers in hand, he lay down by his campfire.

I remained cautious and was becoming rather cold. Apparently understanding my dilemma, the Tamarian rose and took a lighted piece of wood from his fire, and threw it in my direction. After which, we made another attempt to communicate verbally. Despite the fact that our conversation remained mutually unintelligible, I nodded and thanked the Tamarian for the fire. He nodded back as if he understood.

Commander Riker later told me that Worf and his security team were nearing El-Adrel IV's surface when Data read a power surge in the Tamarian ship's plasma reactor. Anticipating that the Tamarian ship was about to fire on our shuttle, Commander Riker immediately ordered Worf to begin an evasive maneuver. Nevertheless, the shuttle was hit. Surprisingly, only the shuttle's starboard thruster was destroyed. Commander Riker ordered Worf to return to the *Enterprise.*

Although this rescue attempt failed, my senior staff was working on alternative strategies. Geordi believed he could increase the transporter's annular confinement beam enough to transport me back through the particle-scattering field the Tamarians had placed around the planet. The more immediate problem was, however, that it would take him a full day to do it, which caused Counselor Troi some concern. By that time, Deanna thought, I might be dead. Worf was less concerned for my immediate safety. It seems he had great confidence in my abilities as a warrior. In his mind, in battle against the Tamarian I would be victorious. In making this observation, Worf assumed that I was involved in a challenge ritual. Others of my senior staff were not so sure, but could only make educated guesses as to the Tamarians' motives— motives that were now less important than my rescue. As such, they continued discussing options for my safe return.

Attacking the Tamarian ship might disable its scattering field and allow the *Enterprise* to beam me back aboard. On the other hand, it remained possible that attacking the Tamarians might start a war, a course of action that Commander Riker was willing to take only when it was the last option available to him.

Data remarked to Mr. Riker that with further study, it still might be possible to find a way to communicate with the Tamarians. Will agreed and asked Deanna to join Data in his research.

Awaking to find the Tamarian gone, I walked over to his campsite, where I found the small objects. I picked one of them up and examined it. Whatever the objects represented totally escaped me. I also found a notebook and studied it.

Meanwhile, despite their efforts, Data and Deanna were reviewing the recordings made of our earlier attempts at conversing with the Tamarians. They concluded that there was some point of contention between the Tamarian captain and his first officer. Data believed the term "Darmok" to be a proper noun, which clearly carried a meaning for the Tamarians. Deanna ordered the computer to search for the term "Darmok" in all linguistic databases for the El-Adrel sector. Forty-seven entries were located; none of their definitions seemed to relate to the Tamarians' use of the term.

Counselor Troi was frustrated that with all the advance technology available to them, they still weren't making any headway. Moreover, although Data had encountered 1,754 nonhuman races in his twenty-six years of service in Starfleet, he, too, was at a loss as to how to say even "Hello" to the Tamarians. Possessing remarkable insight for interacting with human races as well as with many alien cultures, Deanna correctly surmised that a single word, misspoken or misunderstood, could lead to tragedy. Fortunately, neither Data nor Deanna is one who gives up easily. Soon, their perseverance proved fruitful: they were on to something.

On El-Adrel IV, I had just determined the notebook to be some sort of a captain's log, when the Tamarian came running toward me shouting, "Darmok. Darmok and Jalad at Tanagra." Then he said, "Shaka. Temba. His arms wide."

Suddenly, the air filled with a frightful roar. It seemed to come out of nowhere, but everywhere. As he turned in a circle to look around our area, the Tamarian said, "Darmok and Jalad at Tanagra."

With dagger in hand, the Tamarian circled cautiously as if waiting to be attacked. My mind and body filled with fear as the roar rang out once more. Saying, "Temba. His arms wide," the Tamarian offered me one of his daggers. This time, I accepted his offer. Indeed, whatever was making this frightful roar, it was a threat to the both of us.

Meanwhile, a sensor warning sounded on the *Enterprise*. Worf reported to Commander Riker that sensors were picking up an electromagnetic disturbance approaching my position—a variable induction field, possibly a life-form. The field was erratic, appearing and disappearing, but appeared to be moving toward my position and posing to attack. Geordi was two to three hours away from being able to transport me back to the *Enterprise*. Mr. Riker told Geordi to try an alternative approach, one that could be attempted immediately, and ordered O'Brien to stand by to transport.

Daggers in hand, the Tamarian captain and I circled in unison while we waited for the Threat to show itself. Out of the bushes, a nearly invisible creature began to appear before us only to disappear, then reappear to our rear. I tried to tell the Tamarian that we should retreat, but he just shrugged me off and said, "Mirab— his sails unfurled?"

Still, I did not understand, and was trying to get the Tamarian to follow me away from the Threat. But he stood his ground and said, "Shaka. When the walls fell."

Just then, the Threat began to materialize and the Tamarian pushed me aside and took a position to battle our common, unknown foe. Although he seemed to be attempting to protect me, I quickly retook a position by his side. I was not about to allow the Tamarian to face danger alone.

For the moment, the Threat disappeared and the Tamarian said, "Uzani. His army at Lashmir."

As if he could understand my language, I inquired of the Tamarian, "At Lashmir. Was it like this at Lashmir? Similar to what we're facing now?"

Once again we heard a loud crackling sound as the Threat began to materialize, only to disappear once more. The situation was tense. We were both trying to anticipate the Threat's next location and to connect with each other.

The Tamarian said "Uzani . . ." and then took a few steps as if he was trying to distance himself from me. Then he said, "His army. With fist open."

I grew excited as I believed the Tamarian to be communicating a strategy. Opening my hand in gesture, I asked of him, "A strategy? With fist open . . ." Continuing to hold my hand open I probed further, "With fist open. Why . . . ? To lure the enemy . . ."

The Tamarian looked back at me and said, "His army. With fist closed."

I closed my hand and asked, "With fist closed. An army. Open . . . to lure the enemy."

Although I still could not fully understand him, I finally understood that the Children of Tama were a race that communicated by citing examples—communicating in metaphor.

The Tamarian seemed to be very happy and said, "Sokath. His eyes uncovered!"

Indeed, our renewed attempt to communicate was just making progress when the Threat suddenly materialized in the form of an alien creature and attacked. I immediately thrust my dagger into it. Simultaneously, the creature emitted a powerful electrical discharge, which sent me tumbling. The Tamarian then thrust his dagger into the creature. He, too, was immediately knocked away. I made a second attack, only to have the creature strike me with a sweeping blow. By this time, the Tamarian had gotten up and attacked again. He was wrestling with the creature when I felt the familiar, but unexpected, lock-on of a transporter beam. Instinctively, I cried out, "No!" Obviously, no one aboard the *Enterprise* could hear me nor could they know that I wanted to remain on the planet and help my new friend defeat the creature.

Efforts to transport me back aboard the *Enterprise* were unsuccessful—the Tamarian ship's shield was still deflecting the signal, and Geordi couldn't boost the transporter's confinement beam to a level sufficient to override the field's interference. As a result, I was temporarily suspended between the *Enterprise* and the planet's surface.

Just then, Worf reported that sensors indicated that the Tamarian captain and the creature to be in close proximity, and the Tamarian's life signs were fading. Commander Riker was puzzled: what was wrong with the Tamarian crew? Surely their own ship's sensors were showing their captain to be in trouble. Yet they didn't seem to be doing anything to help him get out of the situation.

Opening a communication channel with the Tamarian ship, Commander Riker told them that their captain was in trouble, and asked them to drop their particle field. The Tamarian first officer looked at a sensor panel, uttered something unintelligible, and immediately closed the channel.

Chief O'Brien couldn't hold me in suspension any longer and had to release me from the transporter's confinement beam. As I rematerialized back on the planet's surface, the creature disappeared and I discovered the Tamarian lying on the ground, wounded, but still alive. Not having the strength to rise, the Tamarian managed to say, "Shaka."

I finished the phrase for him, "When the walls fell," just as the Tamarian collapsed.

The situation had turned into a full crisis. Commander Riker was running out of both options and patience. Dr. Crusher detected that my life signs were stable, but the Tamarian's were weakening. Commander La Forge reported that the Tamarian ship had deepened its particle-scattering field; therefore, beaming me back to the *Enterprise* was now out of the question. Attacking the source of the Tamarian ship's particle beam appeared to be the only solution. But knocking out this heavily shielded area couldn't be accomplished with one phaser blast—it would require several direct hits.

Will believed Geordi's new strategy would take too much time. The *Enterprise* needed to strike a single blow to the Tamarian vessel and beam me back up before they knew what was happening. Geordi thought for a moment and told Will that maybe there was a way to do it. But the solution would require Worf's help and several hours to set up. Will immediately put the two of them to work on it.

Despite this new strategy, Commander Riker preferred a peaceful solution to the situation. Although no such solution seemed to be forthcoming, he asked Data and Deanna what they had found out through their study of the Tamarian language. Data reported that the Tamarian ego-structure did not seem to allow what humans normally think of as self-identity. Moreover, the Tamarians seemed to communicate through narrative imagery—a reference to the individuals and places that appeared in their mythohistorical accounts. Deanna added that imagery was everything to the Tamarians, embodying their emotional states . . . their very thought processes. "It's how they communicate and it's how they think."

Will then queried Data and Deanna. If they understood the Tamarian way of thinking, "Shouldn't we be able to get something across with them?"

Data answered the question. "No, sir. The situation is analogous to understanding the grammar of a language but none of the vocabulary." He went on to observe that in order to communicate with the Tamarians, it would first be necessary to understand the imagery from which they draw their relations. Given the situation at the time, such an understanding didn't seem likely.

As nighttime fell upon us, I built a fire and stood watch over the Tamarian captain. Despite his wounds, he was still attempting to communicate with me, and said, "Darmok and Jalad at Tanagra."

He seemed to be referring to our isolation. And I said to him, "Our situation is similar to theirs. I understand. But I need to know more. Tell me more. About Darmok and Jalad. Tell me."

I searched my memory for other words and phrases he had spoken to me.

"You used the words 'Temba. His arms wide' when you gave me the knife and the fire. Could that mean give?" Then I pointed at him and said, "Temba. His arms wide. Darmok. Give me more about Darmok."

The Tamarian looked at me and smiled, then said, "Darmok on the ocean."

At that point, I decided to try a new approach to connect with him. Placing a stone on the ground and drawing a circle around it, I pointed at the stone and said, "Darmok," and then asked if the circle might represent the ocean.

Perhaps it was our mutual patience and imagination that finally made a connection between us. Suddenly, it came to me. "Darmok and Jalad at Tanagra." The Tamarian was playing out a metaphor. He was likening himself to "Darmok" and I represented "Jalad." "Tanagra" was a place where two strangers arrive separately and battled a common enemy—the creature. By struggling together, against this common foe the strangers became friends and left Tanagra together. The Tamarian had hoped something like this would happen. He knew that there was a dangerous creature on this planet, and he knew that a danger shared might sometimes bring two people together.

Finally, we were beginning to communicate. I sensed the dying Tamarian wanted me to tell him a story. Even as my new friend lay dying, I told him a tale familiar to me . . . an Earth story . . . one about two strangers who fight a common foe and become good friends and go on to fight other enemies together. It is, however, a tale with a sad ending. One of them is stricken in battle and dies. As the survivor weeps over the loss of his friend, he ends the story by saying, "He who was my companion through adventure and hardship is gone forever."

Ironically, as I spoke my tale's final words, my

newfound friend also died. In attempting to make new friends for his people, he had given his life. Only then did I understand his sacrifice. Aside from this moment of grief, make no mistake about it—I was still in grave danger.

Meanwhile, on the *Enterprise,* Geordi and Worf had completed their preparations. With no other option available to him, Commander Riker ordered Worf to prepare to fire at the Tamarian ship. Just then, Data informed Mr. Riker that the Tamarian captain's bioscan was becoming unreadable and that he might be dead. Will remarked that if they knew that, so did the Tamarians. Data interrupted and informed Commander Riker that sensors indicated that the creature was closing in on me.

Sure enough, the creature had begun its on-again, off-again materialization. Armed only with one of the Tamarian's daggers, I stood ready to fight to the death.

Precisely the moment the creature began its attack on me, the *Enterprise*'s phasers were fired at the Tamarian vessel, which rendered its particle beam emitters inoperative. The scattering field was down. As the creature leaped toward me, Chief O'Brien activated the transporter and beamed me back to the *Enterprise.* I was safely rescued from the planet, but now we faced another danger.

Commander Riker understood the Tamarians would respond in kind to the *Enterprise*'s attack. Immediately after firing at the Tamarian ship and beaming me back aboard, he ordered shields up, and put the crew on red alert. As anticipated, the Tamarians returned fire. Their volley was well targeted, and partially disabled the *Enterprise*. The *Enterprise* returned fire, and more phaser fire was exchanged. The Tamarian ship's shields held, however, and the *Enterprise*'s shields failed, she could not sustain another hit.

I ran from the transporter room to the bridge and ordered Worf to hail the Tamarian vessel. On the viewscreen, I saw their first officer. He was outraged. Knowing that we could very easily be destroyed, I began to speak with him—repeating metaphors I had learned from his captain. To our great fortune, the Tamarian understood me. We now knew they meant us no harm, nor did we wish them harm. My message understood, the Tamarians ceased their attack and departed the sector.

Truthfully, I don't know if the Children of Tama have become new friends of the Federation, but at least I know they are not our enemies.

Captain's personal journal: Observations on "Communication." Stardate 45071.3. En route to Solarion IV.

Our mission to establish a dialogue with the Tamarians contains many valuable lessons for communicating with races whose language and thought processes are incomprehensible. It also served to confirm other vital principles of effective communication found in everyday life among people who do comprehend each other's language but sometimes fail to understand one another.

Clearly, this mission was very unusual. Our Universal Translators are customarily able to build a translation matrix capable of allowing us to communicate with even previously unencountered life-forms. This mission proved to be a rare exception. It also confirmed a fundamental element of communication: that one cannot rely on technology alone as both the means and the method for establishing meaningful dialogue.

You must also understand that even though "Darmok," the Tamarian captain, sacrificed his own life to achieve communication and a connection with another people, it is extraordinarily rare that one must give up his life to gain an understanding with others. But history is filled with dreadful incidents when a great loss of life resulted from a lack of understanding between two peoples.

I must admit that I initially mistook the Tamarians' action of transporting me to the surface of El-Adrel IV to be one of hostile intent. Thankfully, the Tamarians had no such intentions and used their ship to establish a particle-scattering field around El-Adrel IV, which allowed "Darmok" and "Jalad" sufficient time to begin to understand one another. Indeed, sufficient time for the qualities of patience and imagination to help turn incomprehensible language and ideology into an intelligible form of communication. Oddly enough, even the presence of a deadly, alien creature had a purpose. Indeed, the alien creature was a strange facilitator who served to help us arrive at a way of communicating.

Notwithstanding my knowledge gained while with the Tamarian captain on the planet's surface, I have every confidence that under different circumstances, Data and Troi would have been able to arrive at a way to communicate effectively with the Tamarians.

Commander Riker's actions during this mission were also noteworthy. While there are those who would immediately launch a full-scale attack on an unfamiliar race who had just committed what appeared to be a hostile act, Will continued to attempt to communicate with the Tamarians even though he had to prepare to engage them in combat.

The point of my using this mission to illustrate the importance of communication is to reinforce the plain and simple truth that there are reasons for two different races to have misunderstandings, just as there are reasons why people of the same species, culture, and language sometimes fail to understand one another.

The sense of reality is that as a Starfleet officer, you will normally interact with people whose words and expressions you can understand. But make no erroneous presumptions about it: unless you make a continuing effort to speak in terms others will understand and listen as they speak, there can be no real understanding.

Captain's personal journal: Lessons on "Communication." Stardate 45075.1. En route to Lya Station Alpha.

We have just departed Solarion IV, where we picked up survivors from an apparent Bajoran terrorist attack, and are now en route to Lya Station Alpha. I will use some of our transit time to record what I believe to be important lessons in communication that stem from our encounter with the Children of Tama.

- Broadly considered, effective communication is the single most important element in resolving a crisis situation. Effective communication is also the single most important factor that can prevent a crisis situation.
- To be an effective communicator, you do not always have to agree with other people. However, it is important that you tolerate your differences with them.
- The first battle of most hostile encounters usually begins as the communication process ends. That is true, but it is also true that the last battle ends only after talk resumes.
- Silence is not always golden, but powerful messages can be given without speaking a single word. In other words, what is not spoken is often more important than what is said.
- Judging by body language, tone of voice, facial expressions, and gestures alone, one can often misinterpret people of different cultures and ideology. But this is also true when interacting with people from your own culture, who often share your ideology. For this reason, it is vital that you not allow your nonverbal expression to cause another to misinterpret your message.

- Patience is a quality whose value comes into play when one is attempting to understand another who is having difficulty expressing his thoughts, feelings, opinions, or ideas.
- If one fails to listen to what another is saying, one will often fail to properly respond to what has been said.
- If nothing more, by listening you do learn when another person has very little to say.
- Effective communication does not always lead to agreement. True enough, some of the most effective communications merely result in arriving at the reason why you disagree with the other party.
- Cutting another person off midsentence is generally rude. However, there are times when cutting someone off midsentence is the kindest thing you can do for them at the moment.
- The use of some forms of advanced communications technology inherently removes emotion from what is being said. However, no technology is capable of removing the sting from what has been improperly stated.

And by way of concluding these lessons on communication,

- Always bear in mind that no matter the means by which messages are given or received, your method of communicating must allow messages to be understood. Indeed, effective communication is the lubricant of effective leadership.

I assure you that as a Starfleet officer you can never become an effective leader without being understood or without understanding those upon whom you rely. Make it so.

VI

Politics

"The Continual Price"

Superintendent's foreword to "Politics." *It is easy to underestimate the extremes to which people will go to secure either recognition or reward when they are set against one another. Whether created by intentional design or benign neglect of human nature, dysfunctional politics within organizations creates an environment that impairs productivity and exhausts human spirit. The presence of dysfunctional politics also creates conditions that stimulate all kinds of mind games, backstabbing, coworker sabotage, malicious rumors, finger-pointing, and other power plays only slightly less primitive, but in many ways more barbarous, than combat between gladiators.*

Fortunately, by the mid-twenty-fourth century most, but not all, of the destructive elements of organizational politics had been eliminated from Starfleet. Even so, it is still refreshing to find that on board the Federation's flagship there was neither harmful competition nor deadly consternation to be found among the senior staff. The principal reason for this delightful condition was that Captain Jean-Luc Picard set no quotas on either recognition or reward. Moreover, his "one for all, all for one" operating style granted no allowance for petty jealousy, vile contempt, lack of cooperation, circumventing authority, or rumor-mongering, all of which bring out the worst in people.

However, even on board the Enterprise, *there were occasions when dysfunctioal politics came into play and left something unsettled, something unresolved, and something always to be on the guard for in the future.*

Admiral Andrea Brand
Superintendent, Starfleet Academy

Captain's personal journal: Stardate 44801.2. En route to Kaelon II.

There is a price to be continually paid for being part of Starfleet. The price is being subjected to the worst kind of politics—politics of fear. Let there be no mistake about it, some people who spread fear are not easily identified. They often hide their true selves in a cloak of good deeds. I would like to believe that the people of the Federation have progressed beyond petty differences and, therefore, are immune from playing political games solely for the purpose of spreading fear and destroying the lives of those they target as their victims. However, as a recent incident shows, pious politics pose a constant threat to take away the individual rights of each of us—whether crewman or captain.

* * *

J'Ddan, a Klingon exobiologist, had been aboard the *Enterprise* for several weeks conducting experiments as part of a Federation-Klingon scientific exchange program. During this period, Starfleet Intelligence learned that schematics of the *Enterprise*'s dilithium chamber had fallen into the hands of the Romulans, and an explosion blew the cover off the dilithium chamber and disabled our ship's warp drive. Consequently, the future of the science exchange program was placed in grave jeopardy when suspicions arose that J'Ddan was involved in these acts of espionage and sabotage.

As a first step in attempting to determine if our suspicions were true, I asked Commander Riker and Counselor Troi to question J'Ddan. As a security precaution, Lieutenant Worf also attended the hearing.

Despite evidence that he had accessed top-secret computer files J'Ddan denied any knowledge of the *Enterprise*'s dilithium-chamber schematics being passed on to the Romulans. J'Ddan also denied any involvement in the destruction of our dilithium chamber and believed the only reason for our accusing him of these crimes was his Klingon heritage. Nothing could have been further from the truth.

Regardless of his denials, we knew that J'Ddan had accessed top-secret computer files, but were unable to determine whether or not he was party to either or both criminal acts. Protesting our accusations that he was involved with these crimes, J'Ddan asked to be returned home, if we could not trust him. Commander

Riker informed him that we had already contacted the Klingon High Council and planned to return him home, but not before we had completed our investigation.

Understandably, Starfleet Command was deeply concerned over the situation. For this reason, they brought Admiral Norah Satie out of retirement and dispatched her to the *Enterprise*. She would assist us with our inquiry into these two seemingly related events. Admiral Satie had earned quite a reputation for uncovering conspiracies. It was her investigation that exposed the alien conspiracy against the Federation just three years ago. She arrived aboard our ship in the company of two of her former staff, Sabin Genestra, an aide from Betazed, and Nellen Tore, an assistant from Delb II.

Admiral Satie began her investigation immediately. The explosion had taken place fours days earlier. No one had been killed, but two of our engineering staff had suffered radiation burns. While further investigation would have to wait until our staff could reenter the engine room, Data reported that slow-motion study of the visual log of the explosion indicated that the articulation frame had collapsed. Admiral Satie observed that the schematics of the *Enterprise*'s dilithium chamber, now in Romulan possession, included details of the articulation frame, which was one reason why Starfleet suspected sabotage. Data added that other evidence supported this suspicion. All systems had been operating well within normal parameters until fifty-two milliseconds before the explosion. There had been no indications of any malfunctions.

Back in my ready room, Admiral Satie and I sipped cups of hot tea while we continued our discussion. I was very disturbed over the thought that any Klingon would be providing valuable information to the Romulans. As such, I asked Admiral Satie if Starfleet was aware of any other Klingon-Romulan connections in the recent past. Her answer was of some concern to me, but I didn't react to it. She said that it was not up to her to reveal what Starfleet knew or didn't know about a Klingon-Romulan alliance. I then informed her that we had recently encountered several incidents which might suggest that the Klingons and the Romulans had been developing closer ties. Admiral Satie told me that Starfleet was well aware of these incidents, but rather than discussing them, we should focus on what had just taken place aboard the *Enterprise*.

Just then, Worf came to my ready room carrying a hyposyringe that J'Ddan had been using to treat an illness. Mr. Worf informed us that he believed he had discovered how J'Ddan had carried out his act of espionage. This particular hypospray had been modified with an optical reader that could read information off the *Enterprise*'s isolinear chips. This allowed J'Ddan to extract digital data from our computer, encode it in the form of amino-acid sequences, and transfer them into a fluid. Then by injecting someone with the solution—with or without their knowledge— the information had been transported off the *Enterprise* in the form of inert proteins. Later, the process had been reversed, which allowed this top-secret information to fall into Romulan hands.

Admiral Satie was quite impressed with our security chief's discovery and said that she would like him to be the one who next interrogated J'Ddan. Mr. Worf said that it would be his honor to do so.

As our interrogation of J'Ddan resumed, Worf confronted the Klingon exobiologist with new evidence. Worf had tracked the movements of everyone who had left the *Enterprise* since J'Ddan's arrival. All of their present whereabouts were accounted for—except those of a Tarkanian diplomat who had recently left the *Enterprise* only to later disappear in the Cruses System. J'Ddan said this new evidence was no proof of his guilt.

Worf then confronted J'Ddan with the hypospray found in his quarters. J'Ddan attempted to dismiss the hypospray as necessary for his injections, which controlled a chronic illness. Despite the necessity for such injections, this hypo was not used for that purpose. Worf pointed out to J'Ddan that this particular hypo had been modified with an optical character reader; therefore it was useless for his injections. It had only one function—to transform computer information into biological sequences.

This corroborating evidence caused J'Ddan to suddenly admit his guilt. Indeed, he had stolen top-secret information from the *Enterprise,* but adamantly denied any knowledge of what had caused the explosion. At that point, I ordered Mr. Worf to confine J'Ddan until he could be returned to the Klingons. His own High Council would find a way to punish him for his crime.

Admiral Satie was still not sure of J'Ddan's innocence regarding the explosion. She asked her Betazoid aide, Sabin, what he sensed. Sabin reported that he had no sense that the Klingon was lying about his lack of involvement with the explosion.

Based on this information, I surmised that someone else must be involved. Admiral Satie added that she now believed there to be a bigger problem on my ship than just one Klingon exchange officer. Little did I realize just how strong her appetite for intrigue had become.

In my quarters, the admiral told me that she had seen conspiracies before, and even a specter of conspiracy aboard the *Enterprise* was very frightening to her. I told her that I could scarcely believe it myself and said that I was very grateful to have her aboard. She would surely be able to help us get to the bottom of what was taking place.

Although Starfleet had informed the admiral that we were to work as equals during this investigation, I soon found out that she would break ranks with me and begin a rather despicable witch-hunt on her own—and with Starfleet's consent.

Because of the thoroughness of Worf's investigation leading to J'Ddan's admission of guilt, Admiral Satie and Sabin quickly developed confidence in our security chief's loyalty to the Federation and his abilities as an investigator. They were counting on Worf to be of great assistance in their further investigation.

Admiral Satie still held that J'Ddan must have a fellow conspirator still aboard the *Enterprise.* So we reconvened our informal inquiry. The first witness was Dr. Crusher. Admiral Satie questioned Beverly about her knowledge of J'Ddan's medical treatments. Dr. Crusher was fully aware of J'Ddan's condition, but did not administer his injections herself. This she left up to her assistants.

The next person to be questioned was Crewman First Class Simon Tarses, one of the medical technicians who administered J'Ddan's weekly injections. For reasons that I did not immediately understand, Admiral Satie inquired as to Crewman Tarses's heritage. Mr. Tarses confirmed that he had been born on the Mars colony and that his paternal grandfather was Vulcan. Further probing of this witness revealed that he had given J'Ddan his injections a few times, though other technicians had also given the Klingon injections. Crewman Tarses said he had no further relationship with J'Ddan. I then dismissed the crewman from further questioning.

But as Crewman Tarses left the room, Sabin indicated that he sensed that he was lying, desperately frightened, and hiding something. I acknowledged that while Mr. Tarses seemed clearly frightened, it was hardly reason to believe he was lying or covering something up. Nevertheless, Sabin was relentless in his position. He knew Crewman Tarses was lying about something very serious and jumped to the conclusion that Tarses was the conspirator we were looking for.

Back in my quarters, I informed Admiral Satie that she should not expect me to allow any action against Crewman Tarses solely based on Betazoid intuition.

She responded that Sabin had uncanny instincts, and she had learned to trust them. Despite her trust in him, I told her that I was not happy about her use of this Betazoid. Admiral Satie protested by reminding me that I had a Betazoid counselor and could surely see the advantages of using their instinctive abilities to sense emotions. True enough, but I informed her that in my mind there was a clear difference between a counselor and an investigator. She then asked if I was saying that I had never used Counselor Troi to assist with an investigation. I admitted that I did include Counselor Troi in my investigations, but would never act solely on the basis of her instinct. Admiral Satie then said, "Neither would I." She went on to ask if I would restrict the movement of someone aboard my ship that Counselor Troi had told me was potentially dangerous. I had to admit that I probably would and that I would reevaluate my position on Mr. Tarses.

Then, in a rather scolding voice, Admiral Satie informed me that we should keep our priorities straight. Our job was to uncover a conspiracy and to prevent further damage to the *Enterprise.* Clearly, Mr. Tarses was a suspected saboteur. His movements should be restricted and he should be kept under constant surveillance. I told her that I wanted more evidence before taking such drastic measures. Admiral Satie then informed me that such evidence would be forthcoming. Nevertheless, I informed Admiral Satie that I would not treat Crewman Tarses as a criminal unless there was cause to do so.

Admiral Satie responded to my decision in the

extreme. She began to sternly lecture me on the gravity of the situation and said that I was acting irresponsibly, when, gratefully, her harangue was interrupted by a hail from Commander La Forge. He asked us to come to engineering right away.

Immediately upon our arrival in engineering, we learned the results of Geordi and Data's detailed analysis of what had caused the explosion. They concluded that during the last refitting of the *Enterprise,* the dilithium chamber's articulation frame had been replaced with one that had an undetectable defect. This defective frame had burst under neutron fatigue and resulted in the explosion. There had been no sabotage. The explosion was not intentional. Rather, it was nothing more than an accident.

After departing engineering, we proceeded to the observation lounge and shared this new information with Sabin, Worf, and Nellen. Grimacing with obvious disappointment, Sabin remarked that he found it hard to believe that the explosion was an accident. I assured him that if my crew had arrived at that conclusion, he could be sure that the explosion was an accident. It was then that I became fully aware of Admiral Satie's insatiable desire to continue her investigation. She remarked, "Let us keep our perspective, gentlemen. Just because there was no sabotage doesn't mean that there isn't a conspiracy on this ship. We do have a confessed spy."

Sabin added that J'Ddan had confederates. I asked if he was sure, only to be told by Admiral Satie that it was obvious J'Ddan did. He could not have come aboard the

Federation's flagship and accomplished what he had without help from someone among the crew. I agreed that it would have been difficult, but not impossible.

To say the least, I was taken back when Mr. Worf suggested that we continue to investigate Crewman Tarses. Admiral Satie had now succeeded in planting further suspicions in my own security chief's mind. I reminded those present that Mr. Tarses was innocent until proven guilty. Admiral Satie assured me that their intentions would be to establish his innocence of any wrongdoing, for his own sake. Reluctantly, I agreed to allow Worf and Sabin to continue the investigation, but told them to conclude it as soon as possible.

Later, I went to the room where the hearings were to resume. As I entered the hearing room, I was very disturbed to find that a large crowd had gathered in the gallery. I immediately approached Admiral Satie and quietly asked, "You opened the hearing to spectators?"

She curtly remarked that it was not a good idea to keep hearings closed for too long. Closed hearings create rumors and speculation, and allow spies and saboteurs to avoid the bright lights of open inquiry. I was dismayed, but agreed to continue with the hearings for the moment.

Crewman Tarses was already sitting in the witness chair. For the record, I officially convened the resumption of the hearings. I then informed Mr. Tarses that for his own protection, I had assigned Commander Riker as his counsel. Mr. Tarses thanked me, but said that he needed no protection, he had not done anything wrong.

To my surprise and utter disgust, Admiral Satie began the questioning by asking Dr. Crusher—who was in the gallery, not in the witness chair—if she had observed Crewman Tarses interacting with J'Ddan. Beverly said that she had. She had seen Mr. Tarses administering the Klingon's injections, and she might have seen the two at a social gathering in Ten-Forward. Admiral Satie wanted to interrogate Dr. Crusher further, but I was furious with her line of questioning. I thanked Dr. Crusher for her observations and dismissed her from offering further testimony. Then, I leaned over and told the admiral in no uncertain terms that if she had a case to make against my crewman, she had better make it. Otherwise, I would bring an immediate end to the proceedings.

The Betazoid Sabin then took over the questioning. He first established that Mr. Tarses had unrestricted access to the medical supplies that J'Ddan had used to transport the stolen information off our ship. Then Sabin told Mr. Tarses a blatant lie. He informed Crewman Tarses that there was evidence that the explosion was caused by a corrosive chemical—one he had access to. I was beginning to lose my self-control, but restrained myself enough to allow Sabin to continue questioning the young crewman.

Crewman Tarses testified that he had no part in either incident. Sabin then asked Mr. Tarses how we could believe him when we knew he was a liar. Over Commander Riker's objection that there was no basis for calling the crewman a liar—an objection I agreed with—Sabin assured me that his basis for this accusation was about to become clear. With no further hesitation, Admiral Satie's aide went on to reveal that Simon Tarses had deliberately lied on his personnel application for admission to Starfleet. Crewman Tarses compounded this lie when he had earlier repeated it to our committee. Simon Tarses's paternal grandfather was a Romulan—not a Vulcan! Sabin then asked Mr. Tarses wasn't it Romulan blood he carried and a Romulan heritage that he honored? Heeding the advice of his counsel, Crewman Tarses refused to answer Sabin's question on the basis that the answer might incriminate him.

Now, Sabin's line of questioning had made me very angry. I called a recess to the proceedings. It would allow everyone to calm down and give me the opportunity to regain control of the situation.

I returned to my ready room only to find Worf instructing members of his security staff to conduct an even more thorough investigation of Crewman Tarses's past. I interrupted and told Mr. Worf I needed to talk with him.

Somewhat puzzled by the enthusiasm he was displaying for this investigation, I asked my security chief if he was aware of what was happening aboard our ship. He didn't know what I was getting at. I told him it was not unlike the Drumhead trials of five hundred years ago. In these proceedings military officers would upend a drum on the battlefield, sit on it, and dispense summary justice. Their decisions were quick and their punishments severe. I told him if we let our present situation become a Drumhead, we would all be doomed.

Worf protested. We had a confessed conspirator in J'Ddan, and Tarses had all but admitted his own guilt. I asked Mr. Worf just how Crewman Tarses had indicated his guilt. Worf said by refusing to answer Sabin's question about his Romulan grandfather. Not only did Worf's rationale alarm me, I was now furious with him as well. I shouted back that refusing to answer a question is not a crime, nor could we infer Crewman Tarses's guilt because he refused to respond to Sabin's question!

Worf then shouted back, "Captain, if a man were not afraid of the truth, he would answer!"

"Oh no," I said. "We cannot allow ourselves to think that."

I continued by reminding Mr. Worf that the *seventh guarantee* is one of the most important rights in the Federation's constitution. It protects our people against self-incrimination. We could not allow ourselves to take this fundamental right and turn it against a citizen.

Emphatically, he responded that the Federation had enemies and it was our duty to seek them out.

Worf's zeal to find a conspirator—where one was not to be found—dismayed me even more. I said to him, "Oh yes, that's how it starts. But the road from . . . legitimate suspicion to rampant paranoia is very much shorter than we think."

Clearly, Worf was unconvinced. He had been duped by Admiral Satie and her able aide. Worf was caught up in their zealous, self-imposed quest to make a conspirator out of someone, even an innocent man. Little did I know that they would soon turn their inquisition on me.

I couldn't tolerate the situation any longer. Something very wrong was taking place on my ship, and I didn't like it. Leaving Worf sitting there, I rose and went to visit with Crewman Tarses.

As we sipped tea, Mr. Tarses told me that all his life he had wanted to be part of Starfleet. He had attended Starfleet Academy's program for enlisted personnel and successfully passed the course for medical technicians. After duty on several outposts, he had been selected for service aboard the *Enterprise.* It had been the happiest day of his life. Although he assured me that he was innocent of the charges being brought against him, he thought his career was over because he had lied on his application. As Crewman Tarses finished speaking, a pang of great sorrow filled my heart. Things had gone too far. I had to restore order to my ship.

Concluding my visit with Mr. Tarses, I immediately found Admiral Satie and told her of my conversation with Crewman Tarses. An admission that he had lied on his application to Starfleet did not make him a traitor. She was hounding an innocent man and it must stop. I could not allow it to go on.

The admiral thought me naive. She had spent the last four years of her life going from starship to starbase, uncovering conspiracy after conspiracy. Consequently, she had no home, no friends. But these things didn't matter to her; she had a greater purpose in life. Indeed, although she had once been a fine officer in Starfleet, Admiral Satie's purpose in life had now become to prevent anyone from destroying the Federation. When she had finished making her point, I told her that the hearings on Mr. Tarses would stop. If she did not agree, I would go to Starfleet.

Admiral Satie then proudly told me it was too late. She had been in constant contact with Starfleet Command. The hearings were not only going to proceed, they were going to be expanded. She was going to get to the heart of the conspiracy, even if it meant investigating every member of my crew. Moreover, Admiral Thomas Henry of Starfleet Security, with whom she had worked closely in the past, was on his way to observe the remainder of the proceedings. She had personally requested his presence. Admiral Satie informed me she didn't need my permission or approval for taking this action—she reported to Starfleet directly.

There may be something more disturbing to a starship captain than to have his authority usurped by someone from Starfleet Command, but I was at a loss at that moment to think of one. Despite my anger, I had to maintain some composure if I was to regain control of my ship. As Admiral Satie left my ready room, I told her that what she was doing was unethical and immoral, and I was going to fight it. Undaunted, Admiral Satie said, "Do what you must, Captain . . . so will I."

Back on the bridge, Data informed me that our warp engines were repaired. And he was ready to begin restart sequences. A few moments later, Nellen entered the bridge. With a smug smirk, she handed me a padd containing orders for me to appear before the investigation committee the following morning. I was a little puzzled, but not surprised, by this summons.

By the next morning, Admiral Henry had arrived. Over the protest of Admiral Satie, I began my testimony with a statement.

My statement was one of deep concern over what was happening—something that began when we apprehended a spy. J'Ddan had admitted his guilt and would be punished by the Klingon High Council for his crime. But the hunt for a conspirator didn't end there. Crewman Tarses, an innocent man, was then brought to trial without any evidence that he had committed a crime. Because his grandfather was Romulan, Mr. Tarses's career was now in ruins. I asked the committee, "Have we become so . . . fearful . . . have we become so cowardly . . . that we must extinguish a man because he carries the blood of a current enemy?"

I went on to ask Admiral Satie to let us not condemn Mr. Tarses or anyone else because of their bloodlines, or to investigate others because of their innocent associations. That said, I implored her to stop the proceeding.

Admiral Satie gave no regard to my plea. Instead, she immediately began questioning my loyalty to the Prime Directive and reminded me that I had violated it on nine previous occasions—the circumstances of which I had thoroughly and truthfully reported to Starfleet Command. But this fact didn't satisfy Admiral Satie's passion to reveal the true conspirator on the *Enterprise*—me.

Sabin continued this line of questioning by asking

me about an incident that had taken place when, following orders, I transported a Vulcan ambassador to a location near the Neutral Zone. As it turned out, the ambassador was not Vulcan, she was a Romulan spy. Admiral Satie joined in and asked if, once her true identity became known to me, had I taken any action to retrieve the Romulan spy, who was carrying Federation secrets she had been accumulating for years. I admitted that I had made no such effort.

Worf jumped to his feet and protested the admiral's inference. He shouted out that I had taken the appropriate action to prevent the *Enterprise* from being captured by the Romulans. Admiral Satie immediately turned on Worf. She asked where he had been when this traitor was on the *Enterprise*. Why hadn't ship's security taken action? Clearly, she was now including Mr. Worf as another Romulan conspirator.

Sabin added to the admiral's insult by asking if I thought it was questionable judgment to have a security officer aboard my ship whose father was a Romulan collaborator. True enough, the Klingon High Council had convicted Worf's father, Mogh, of treason at Khitomer. But the evidence against Mogh had been falsified by the politically powerful Duras family. Moreover, the Klingon High Council had subsequently refused to hear new evidence that revealed this deception. Indeed, Mogh had been no less a victim of a Drumhead trial than had been many soldiers on battlefields centuries ago. Worf was so enraged that he was about to attack Sabin when I motioned him to stop.

Relentlessly, Admiral Satie began a new line of

interrogation. She asked if I had completely recovered from my experience with the Borg and went on to say how awful it must have been for me to know that the Borg had used my knowledge during their attack on Earth—an attack that destroyed thirty-nine starships and killed some eleven thousand of our people. She wondered how I could sleep at night after being responsible for so much destruction. Never mind that all her allegations were entirely false, she had directly challenged my loyalty to the Federation.

I then recalled some words about freedom—words that her own father had once written as wisdom and warning. ". . . The first time any man's freedom is trodden on, we're all damaged."

On hearing me quote her father, Admiral Satie lost all control and lashed out at me with unbridled rage. How dare I, one who consorted with Romulans, invoke her father's wisdom to support my traitorous arguments! Her father was a great man and loyal to the Federation. I dirtied his name by using it. She was going to expose me for what I was in her mind—a traitor!

Admiral Henry had been silently observing the proceedings and had now obviously heard enough, as he rose and left the hearing room without comment. Sabin then suggested that it might be an appropriate time for a recess until the next day.

I went to the observation lounge to collect my thoughts. Worf soon joined me and informed me that Admiral Henry had called an end to any more hearings on the matter. Admiral Satie and her staff had left the

Enterprise. Worf then admitted that he had been beguiled by the admiral. He had believed and even helped her. He did not see her for what she was, but now that she had been exposed, Admiral Satie might not be so trusted in the future.

I said, "Maybe." Then I told my trusted security chief that Admiral Satie, or someone like her, would always be with us, lying in wait for the right climate in which to flourish by spreading fear in the name of righteousness.

Captain's personal journal: Observations on "Politics." Stardate 44815.3. Departing Kaelon II.

While the Federation's progress often results from the actions of those possessed by an undaunted zeal to achieve their purposes, its progress is indeed damaged when even one of its people is zealously and wrongly prosecuted for crimes he didn't commit. Perhaps this explains why I was truly dismayed by Admiral Satie's recent actions aboard my ship. Although she had once placed confidence in both my ability to command and my loyalty to the Federation by issuing the order that placed me in command of its flagship, Admiral Satie's recent actions were clear indications that she was quite willing to disregard that fact as well as any inconvenient truth in order to expose a conspiracy aboard the *Enterprise.*

As she did expose her real self during the investigation, I doubt that Admiral Satie will be trusted by Starfleet Command in the future. I now have to wonder if Admiral Satie had turned innocent people into victims during her previous successes in exposing conspiracies against the Federation. And though Admiral Satie was once considered to be a fine and distinguished officer of the Starfleet, all of her past accomplishments will now be remembered with far less accuracy and frequency than will her mean-spirited, pointless, and baseless witch-hunt to expose a conspiracy where there was none to be found.

Sabin and Nellen proved to be either oblivious to Admiral Satie's real intention or willing accomplices to it. Whatever the case, Sabin's Betazoid ability to sense feelings became a powerful foil by which Admiral Satie probed for conspirators. Obviously, Nellen did no harm by simply recording the proceedings and performing other administrative duties for one who had once earned, and perhaps deserved, her loyalty. Notwithstanding the reason for their supporting Admiral Satie in her unremitting quest to expose yet another conspiracy, I can only hope that Sabin and Nellen's example will be a lesson that enables others to distinguish between the merits of legitimate loyalty and the pitfalls of blind obedience.

Allowing the Klingon High Council to deal with J'Ddan's violation of the Federation-Klingon treaty was politically appropriate. I have every confidence that J'Ddan has been severely punished for providing the Romulans with a copy of the schematics of the *Enter-*

prise's dilithium chamber. We can only hope that this top-secret information never becomes a strategic advantage for the Romulans to use against us.

While I understand Crewman Tarses's reason for lying on his application to Starfleet, I do not condone it. Quite simply, a Starfleet officer's first duty is to the truth, and such duty also extends to every crewman and technician. As Mr. Tarses has also proven himself to be a valuable member of my crew and has been honest in all other matters, I am willing to forgive him for this mistake and have recommended to Starfleet that he be retained in its service. Regardless, I do hope that Simon Tarses's bloodlines will never again be the reason for others to drum up charges against him.

Understandably, Admiral Satie's recent success in uncovering other conspiracies had earned Admiral Henry's confidence in her abilities to investigate suspected crimes against the Federation. When Admiral Henry came aboard the *Enterprise* to observe and oversee the expansion of Admiral Satie's investigation, he could have taken charge and conducted the proceedings himself. However, by allowing Admiral Satie to conduct the proceedings, under his watchful eye, Admiral Henry was able to witness for himself that she had crossed over the line of reason and that she had become a disruptive force within the Starfleet.

Because Mr. Worf is responsible for our ship's security and discovered J'Ddan to have committed an act of espionage, it was only logical that Admiral Satie would want him to assist Sabin with the investigation of a possible conspiracy. Indeed, I was rather disturbed to learn Mr. Worf was so caught up in Admiral Satie's Drumhead trial, that he was quite willing to disregard Mr. Tarses's constitutional right to refuse to answer a question. More importantly, Mr. Worf lacked experience in dealing with a senior Starfleet officer like Admiral Satie, who was so able to deceive others by masking her real intentions. I am confident that Mr. Worf will not be easily deceived in the future. So despite his miscalculations, this event was a tremendous learning experience for Mr. Worf, and I now have even greater confidence in him.

This event caused considerable disruption aboard the *Enterprise,* but as my crew is a resilient one, we have paid the price for being exposed to politics of fear and are now fully refocused on our continuing mission.

Captain's personal journal: Lessons on "Politics." Stardate 44820.1. En route to Peliar Zel.

There is no denying that politics are the means by which civilized people conduct their affairs. Civilized conduct also helps people smooth out the occasional wrinkles that emerge in relationships aboard a starship. Well-intentioned and functional politics are vital to the governance of organizations and the people who serve them.

However, there is an ever-present potential in all of us to reveal the dark side of power and authority. As Starfleet officers, you are expected to do nothing less than keep such dysfunctional behavior under control. For this purpose, I offer you the following lessons.

- Aboard a starship, rules of conduct create an atmosphere of decency by controlling irrationality.

- An officer who seeks to distinguish himself at the expense of the innocent should first dig two graves. Indeed, wrongful destruction of another person's reputation will soon become the death of one's own.

- It is possible that even the most notable officer may become so weakened by flattery that he ceases to cultivate his authority properly, ceases to acknowledge fact, ceases to heed honest criticism . . . until someday he finds himself deserted by those who once trusted him.

- Indeed, an officer who emphasizes those things his crew share in common, and who has the ability to help them understand what may keep them apart, equips his crew with a great deal of ability to control their own irrationality.

- An officer who constantly seeks to find fault in others does not always succeed. Nevertheless, in doing so, one usually causes them harm and creates an environment of distrust for everyone.

- While an officer may not always be persuaded to act on fact, he should never allow himself to be corrupted by the zeal to gain his own ends despite what is truth.

- A person's bloodlines are a condition of birth and are neither cause for alleging him guilty of crimes nor reason for disqualifying him from becoming a member of Starfleet. We must recognize that if humanity is to make improvement, we must respect the right of all people to have an unencumbered part in our progress.

- Although an officer has every right to expect his crew to follow lawful orders, no officer has the authority to compel any member of the crew to become part of his illegal activity or abuses of his power.

- Bear in mind that an officer who respects the authority and power that attend his office exercises them in devotion to his duty to help others succeed.

- No officer or groups of officers can ever completely prevent others from sowing seeds of fear, doubt, and distrust. Consequently, every officer ought to stand prepared to boldly uproot any seeds so sown by any officer.

And in conclusion,

- Make no mistake, political games never end and are never totally resolved to everyone's satisfaction. Indeed, there is always something that remains unsettled, always something left unsaid, and always someone ready to replace those people exposed for creating dysfunction within the organization.

Everyone pays a price for those who would spread fear in the name of self-righteousness or who would otherwise create distrust, suspicion, and fear among the crew. Protecting individual rights is a continual price for being part of the Starfleet. It is a price that an officer should willingly pay lest he become corrupted himself. Indeed, there is no success worth sacrificing the individual rights of any person, and no reason why one person's corrupted ambitions need corrupt those of others. Make it so.

VII

Intellectual Honesty

"Code of Honor"

Superintendent's foreword to "Intellectual Honesty." *The desire people have to place their trust in the words and deeds of their leaders is nothing new to those living in the twenty-fourth century. Intellectual honesty has always been greatly admired, in both leader and follower.*

The failure of some leaders and followers to estimate the true value other people place on their words and deeds has always accounted for the lack of integrity in social, political, military, and business life. Although corrupt, the intellectually dishonest are not fools. They mask their dishonesty in half-truths, false promises, and other deceptive practices. Nevertheless, they are usually found out. Moreover, they never completely honor their own life or the lives of those they lead astray. The great sadness here is that there is no justifiable reason for intellectual dishonesty, and its transient rewards have no lasting value.

Those who served aboard the Enterprise *were people of the highest personal integrity. True to his convictions, Captain Picard set the example for all to follow. His was an infectious example, which caused the crew of the* Enterprise *to place their full trust and confidence in him. Likewise, Captain Picard placed his full trust and confidence in his crew. Simply said, the* Enterprise *maintained an environment free from the vicious cycle of doubt and distrust that lingers in workplaces where intellectual dishonesty is tolerated.*

Indeed, whatever consequences the truth may bear, the captain and the crew of the Federation's flagship maintained the highest standards of truth. For them, intellectual honesty was their "code of honor."

Admiral Andrea Brand
Superintendent, Starfleet Academy

Captain's personal journal: Stardate 46381.7. Departing the Minos Korva star system.

Recent events have brought me a great deal of personal suffering and humiliation. My senior staff and crew were placed in jeopardy and subjected to senseless humiliation as well. I am now relieved to report that life on board the *Enterprise* is now back to normal. Nevertheless, these events illustrate the importance intellectual honesty has in a Starfleet officer's life. You must also understand that I am not given to open criticism of senior officers, or anyone else for that matter, but I believe that it is my responsibility to be open and frank with you in this record, and will proceed on that basis.

Starfleet requested us to rendezvous with the *U.S.S. Cairo* near the Cardassian border for an urgent meeting with Vice-Admiral Nechayev. No sooner had Commander Riker introduced us than Admiral Nechayev summarily dismissed him and informed me that she had come to relieve me of command of the *Enterprise*. Completely unexpected, her message stunned me.

Admiral Nechayev also informed me that Dr. Crusher and Lieutenant Worf would be joining me on an away team charged with a secret mission, so secret that I was ordered not to discuss its details with them, even as we prepared for it by undergoing commando-style training in one of the *Enterprise*'s holodecks. To be sure, this order directly conflicted with my way of leading.

Let there be no doubt about it, I was truly dismayed by Admiral Nechayev's refusal to listen to alternative suggestions for conducting this mission. Granted, her approach to the problem was certainly an option, but not the only one.

As soon as I departed to begin training my away team, Admiral Nechayev summoned Commander Riker, Commander Data, and Counselor Troi to a briefing, where she informed them that the Cardassian forces, recently withdrawn from the Bajoran sector, were now redeployed along the Federation border. Additionally, the Cardassian Union had mobilized three divisions of ground troops and increased its subspace communications by fifty percent. Based on these activities, Starfleet Command believed the Cardassians to be preparing for an incursion into Federation space.

A recent Starfleet Intelligence report had suggested that the Cardassians were preparing to seize Minos

Korva, one of the disputed systems along the Federation-Cardassian border. The Cardassians were gambling that the Federation would not go to war over one system. Hoping to avoid such a decision, Starfleet was ordering the *Enterprise* to be deployed along the Cardassian border. They believed the presence of the Federation's flagship would send the Cardassian Union a message about the seriousness of the situation. Starfleet Command had also decided to open talks with the Cardassians. The *Enterprise* was to meet with the Cardassians' representative near their border.

Puzzled by my absence from this briefing, Commander Riker inquired as to my whereabouts. Admiral Nechayev told him and the others of my senior staff that their captain, chief medical officer, and security chief had been reassigned. That was all she could tell them for the time being. She then informed the crew that she was giving Captain Edward Jellico command of the *Enterprise* later that afternoon. Admiral Nechayev told them that two years ago, Captain Jellico had helped negotiate the original Federation-Cardassian armistice. It was her opinion that he was the most qualified man to lead this mission. The change of command was to take place at 1300 hours. That said, she ended her briefing.

As I later learned, Will waited until Data and Deanna had left the room and then respectfully expressed his opinion that it was not necessary to give Captain Jellico command of the *Enterprise* just to conduct a negotiation. The admiral told Commander Riker that she disagreed. The *Enterprise* would be in a very dangerous position and she wanted someone on the bridge who had a great deal of experience with the Cardassians. With great indifference to Commander Riker's outstanding record and leadership ability, but saying she meant no offense to him, the admiral simply told him, "That's not you."

Commander Riker proceeded to a transporter room, where he welcomed Captain Jellico aboard the *Enterprise*. Despite not having any experience aboard a Galaxy-class starship and being unknown to my crew, from the moment he beamed aboard and even before he had officially assumed command of my ship, Captain Jellico began a rapid-fire ordering of changes in the *Enterprise*'s standard duty watches, and making demands for detailed information and status reports.

After the change of command ceremony, I attempted to provide my successor with some information about the *Enterprise* that I thought he would find useful. As I soon found out, Captain Jellico just wanted me to get out of his way. He had his own way of doing things and gave no consideration as to what burdens his demands might place on the crew. Quite frankly, the *Enterprise*'s new captain sought no one's opinion nor did he want his orders questioned. He just wanted things done—his way and now.

Oddly enough for someone who was supposedly being sent to conduct open talks to peacefully ease the tension building between the Federation and the Cardassians, once the *Enterprise* was under way to the border, Captain Jellico began ordering modifications to be made in the ship's power, computer, and weapons configuration. Despite being informed that some of his desired changes were contrary to the design specifications of Galaxy-class starships, such technicalities were irrelevant—the *Enterprise*'s present configurations were just not good enough for him. Captain Jellico reasoned that if the talks with the Cardassians failed, the *Enterprise* could find herself in a war zone, and if that happened, he wanted to be "loaded for bear." Additionally, he ordered Commander Riker to personally supervise a battle drill for each shift—drills simulating a series of attacks by a Cardassian squadron.

Sensing the effect that the change in command was having on the crew's morale, Counselor Troi asked Captain Jellico's permission to speak with him. Granting permission, Captain Jellico told her that he had noticed some resistance among the crew. Deanna told her new captain that she wouldn't call it resistance, but uncertainty. Most of the crew had served under my command for several years. As a result, they knew me and what I expected of them. Now the crew was being asked to adjust to a new captain and a new way of doing things, and they were uncertain how to react.

Captain Jellico thanked Counselor Troi for bringing her concerns to his attention. He said that he could see how this could be "unsettling." Deanna observed that it could be equally unsettling to him; perhaps everyone just needed a little time to make the adjustment. While agreeing with Counselor Troi in principle, Captain Jellico informed her that unfortunately he didn't have time for a "honeymoon" with the crew and instructed Deanna to take charge of the morale situation. Indeed,

Counselor Troi was to make sure that the crew made the adjustment to the new routine easily and quickly.

Just before my away team departed the *Enterprise,* I met with Captain Jellico to go over the orders for my mission. Our conversation was interrupted when Mr. Riker hailed Captain Jellico to announce that we had arrived at the coordinates for my away team's shuttle departure. Captain Jellico asked Commander Riker if he had launched the probe that he had requested—a probe that would provide me with current intelligence information for my mission. Mr. Riker affirmed that he had, but said he was unaware that Captain Jellico wanted to be so informed. Captain Jellico ended their communication and remarked that it was no wonder Will Riker had been a first officer for so long a time. I informed him that Commander Riker was still a first officer by choice. A highly decorated officer, Commander Riker had been offered his own command by Starfleet on more than one occasion. If only given a chance, Commander Riker would prove himself to be an outstanding officer. It was at this moment when Captain Jellico exposed more of his true character to me. Speaking candidly, Captain Jellico said he didn't believe that I would return from my mission alive. He had no faith that the talks with the Cardassians would be successful; the Federation just wasn't going to give in to their demands. Moreover, he didn't have time to give Will Riker or anyone else a chance. And speaking bluntly, the *Enterprise* was now under his command.

Obviously, Captain Jellico was an officer who had many fine points; otherwise he would not have advanced to the rank of a Starfleet captain. To me, however, it was just as obvious that diplomacy was not one of them.

Once under way on the shuttlecraft, I was authorized to inform Beverly and Worf on the precise purpose of our mission. Starfleet Intelligence believed the Cardassians to be secretly developing a new delivery system for metagenic weapons. This new delivery system would allow dormant, genetically engineered viruses to be transmitted on a theta-band subspace carrier wave. The weapon was designed to activate the viruses after launch, which would prevent the Cardassians from accidentally exposing themselves to active metagenic agents.

I was familiar with such weapons. They are designed to destroy entire ecosystems and life-forms within a few days after release. In a month, the metagenic agent itself breaks down and dissipates completely, leaving every city, road, and every piece of equipment perfectly intact. An intergalactic treaty had outlawed such weapons of destruction several years earlier; even the Romulans were abiding by this agreement.

Theta-band subspace carrier-wave emissions had been recently detected as coming from Celtris III, but we knew very little about this planet. It was thought to be uninhabited until these emissions were detected. Starfleet Intelligence believed the Cardassians had a lab located somewhere beneath the planet's surface where they were secretly developing this dreadful weapon. Our orders were to penetrate this installation and find out if the Cardassians were actually developing this weapon. If they were, our job was to destroy it—at any cost.

While captain of the *Stargazer*, I had conducted extensive tests of theta-band waves. This experience was one of the reasons why I was selected for this mission. Dr. Crusher's role was to locate and destroy any biotoxins we found. Worf's role was obvious.

Celtris III is located in Cardassian space. Getting there safely would not be easy, and if detected, our unauthorized presence on this planet would be considered a violation of the Federation-Cardassian peace agreement. However, I knew of a way to arrange for some discreet transportation to Celtris III, and we set a course for Torman V.

On arrival at Torman V, we made our way to a local bar filled with even more despicable characters than I remember patronizing the Bonestell Recreational Facility. We made contact with DaiMon Solok, a Ferengi smuggler whose lack of scruples allowed him to profit from doing business on both sides of the border in this sector. It was Solok's lack of scruples that allowed Beverly to manipulate him into transporting our away team to Celtris III.

Once my away team arrived at Celtris III, we quickly located the entry to a rather deep and long tunnel, which led to the secret lab where the Cardassians were developing the metagenic weapon.

Meanwhile, the *Enterprise* had rendezvoused with the Cardassian spaceship *Reklar* to begin diplomatic talks. Gul Lemec, the Cardassian representative, beamed aboard the *Enterprise* only to have Captain

Jellico make him wait in the observation lounge for over an hour before joining him. Captain Jellico told Commander Riker and Counselor Troi that making him wait would show the Cardassian just who was in control. You may consider this a juvenile negotiating tactic, as I do. However, this ploy would be just the beginning of Captain Jellico's power plays with the Cardassian representative.

Gul Lemec believed that just he and Captain Jellico would be involved in these negotiations, which explains why he was surprised that Captain Jellico had Commander Riker and Counselor Troi accompany him to the talks. Cunningly so, Captain Jellico thought that their numbers would cause the Cardassian to be more cautious in making his demands. However, such was not the case. Being left to await the arrival of the Federation's representative to the talks just insulted the Cardassian envoy, and he protested Commander Riker and Counselor Troi's presence at the meeting. Captain Jellico quickly turned Lemec's protest against him. He told the Cardassian envoy that his concerns were nothing more than minutiae—a sign that he wasn't being serious about the talks. If the Cardassian Union was truly interested in discussing peace, maybe they would send someone who would participate in a civilized manner. That said, Captain Jellico abruptly left the observation lounge.

Back on the bridge, Captain Jellico instructed Will and Deanna to let the Cardassian stew for a few minutes then return and tell him that their captain was agreeable to one more meeting. But as Jellico was a loose cannon and unreasonable, Gul Lemec would have to be more reasonable in making his demands.

When the talks resumed, Gul Lemec had been joined by two aides. Unfortunately, the negotiations quickly turned into an exchange of accusations. The Federation believed the massing of Cardassian troops and spacecraft along the border to be a provocation of war. Gul Lemec said the Cardassians were simply conducting training exercises. Nevertheless, he demanded that the Federation concede the disputed territories.

Gul Lemec then said that he had heard a rumor that the Federation had sent a small team into Cardassian territory. Captain Jellico denied knowing anything about this rumor. Despite this denial, Gul Lemec was fully aware of our away team's presence on Celtris III—a Cardassian planet. As the Cardassians had not given us permission to be there, our mission to Celtris III was a violation of the armistice and an act of war. Suggesting a brief recess in the talks, Gul Lemec made it clear he knew I was part of the team the Federation had sent to Celtris III. As we were to soon discover, the Cardassians had only led the Federation to believe that they were developing a new metagenic weapon. Correctly anticipating that I would be part of the team sent to investigate, the development of a metagenic weapon was a ruse. What the Cardassians were actually doing was setting a trap—for me.

Once inside the door to the "secret lab," we discovered that no one was working there. In fact, there was no lab. Before we could escape, we were attacked by a small group of Cardassian soldiers. Phaser blasts were exchanged, and we fought them in hand-to-hand combat. To our great misfortune, we were outnumbered and I was taken prisoner, but Beverly and Worf managed to escape. As my rescue was beyond their present abilities, Dr. Crusher and Lieutenant Worf began making their way to the prearranged rendezvous point, where they would be picked up by a shuttle and safely returned to the *Enterprise.*

Back on the *Enterprise,* Commander Riker informed Captain Jellico that the ship's sensors had picked up a series of coded messages coming from Celtris III and could only detect residual theta-band emissions. Captain Jellico assumed that this signal was a sign that one way or another we had completed our mission, and he informed Admiral Nechayev. Nevertheless, they were aware neither of my away team's present whereabouts nor if we were alive.

Meanwhile, I was taken to a facility where a Cardassian captain by the name of Gul Madred interrogated me about the Federation's plans for defending Minos Korva. Believing that, as captain of the *Enterprise,* I would be fully informed of these plans, they had designed an elaborate ruse to capture me. Unfortunately for them, the Federation's plans were transmitted to the *Enterprise* only after my away team had departed for its mission, which meant I could not tell the Cardassians what they wanted to know even though they injected me with some sort of truth serum.

The Cardassians sent a message to Gul Lemec informing him of my capture. Gul Lemec apprised Captain Jellico that I had been taken captive. Gul Lemec then added some disinformation as to what had taken place on Celtris III and told Captain Jellico that the Cardassian Union hadn't yet decided how they would react to this provocation, but they would respond.

Publicly maintaining his lack of any knowledge regarding any Federation team being sent into Cardassian space, Captain Jellico privately divulged his knowledge of our mission to Commander Riker and Counselor Troi. As he was not one to take the Cardassians at their word, Captain Jellico dispatched Mr. Riker in a shuttlecraft to our prearranged rendez-vous point in the Lyshan System—just in case we had escaped.

Meanwhile, Gul Madred began to pursue another agenda with me—a game of will and submission. He told me that if I would cooperate by telling him the Federation's defense plans for Minos Korva, my punish-ment as a spy would be . . . civilized. Clearly, as he had interrogated me while I was under the influence of a truth serum, Gul Madred was fully aware that I knew nothing about these plans. No matter, this truth did not prevent him from subjecting me to brutal torture. Stripped of my clothing and bound by my wrists, I was suspended from the ceiling throughout the night. On awakening, I learned that the Cardassians had im-planted a device in my chest—a device that could direct the most excruciating pain to any part of my body.

Madred returned the next morning and admitted that he was sure that I had told him everything I knew. But, it was not enough. Now he was going to accomplish what *he* had intended from the beginning—getting me to submit to him. It was a test of wills.

The Cardassian then turned on four bright lights, which were aimed directly into my face, and asked me what I saw. I told him, "Four lights."

Gul Madred said no, "There are five."

As I would not agree that there were five lights, Gul Madred activated the device implanted in my chest. The pain was unbearable, but I was determined not to allow him to possess my mind. To be certain, I paid a painful price for my resistance as Gul Madred sent another jolt of extraordinary pain riveting through my body.

The Cardassians had made a recording of my confession and sent a copy to Gul Lemec, who showed it to Captain Jellico. Telling Gul Lemec that I was not acting under his orders, Captain Jellico said my fate was of no concern to him. Gul Lemec told Captain Jellico that if the Federation would agree to withdraw from the Minos Korva sector, I would be released unharmed. Otherwise, I would be treated as a terrorist and quite possibly executed. Captain Jellico said he would have to discuss this matter with his superiors. Gul Lemec gave Captain Jellico seven hours to decide what the Federation's answer to his offer would be.

Privately, Captain Jellico told Commander Riker to send a message to Admiral Nechayev recommending that she reject Lemec's proposal. Will then asked Captain Jellico what he intended to do about me. Captain Jellico shook his head, indicating nothing. Mr. Riker then told Captain Jellico that while he was not suggesting that the Federation give up a star system just to save one man's life, the least Captain Jellico could do was to acknowledge that I was acting under Federation orders, which would at least allow me to be treated as a prisoner of war. Captain Jellico said he would not make such an admission; it would be a sign of weakness in the negotiations.

Mr. Riker was outraged that Captain Jellico was willing to sacrifice me as a negotiation tactic. As Will was the *Enterprise*'s first officer, it was his responsibility to point out any actions that may be mistakes by her commanding officer. Indeed, Will disagreed with Captain Jellico's refusal to inform the Cardassians that I was acting under Federation orders. But as Captain Jellico had previously shown himself closed to suggestions and was no longer open to criticism—right or wrong—he immediately relieved Commander Riker of his duties. A few minutes later, Captain Jellico appointed Data as the *Enterprise*'s first officer.

Based on his analysis of the events of the past few days, Data reported that he believed that the Cardassians were planning on launching an attack in the Minos Korva sector. Captain Jellico directed Commander La Forge to try and find out where. Using sensors to analyze Gul Lemec's ship's hull, Geordi found evidence that it was quite possible that the Cardassians were hiding their invasion fleet inside the McAllister Nebula—well inside Cardassian territory, but only eleven light-years from Minos Korva. Geordi also surmised that the Cardassians could only remain inside the cloud for another seventeen hours without sustaining damage to their ships' hulls. Based on Geordi's conclusions, Captain Jellico told Data he wanted to be at Minos Korva in one hour.

Meanwhile, Gul Madred continued to torment and torture me. Believe me, it was a difficult struggle to keep from telling Gul Madred that there were indeed "five lights." Then, quite unexpectedly, Gul Madrid admitted that since he could not break me, he could see no point in keeping me further. I was free to go. As I rose and began making my way across the room, my interrogator said that the Cardassians would get what they wanted from the human female—Worf had been killed while attempting to escape, but Dr. Crusher had been taken alive, or so he led me to believe. Fearing that Beverly would be subjected to as much torture as I had been—and possibly more—I choose to remain behind, which seemed to please Gul Madred as it would allow him to continue our war of wills.

Meanwhile, Captain Jellico had gained Admiral Nechayev's approval to launch a preemptive strike against the Cardassian fleet hiding inside the McAllister Nebula. His senior staff did not agree with this decision, which did not bother Captain Jellico at all. As such, Captain Jellico just ordered his staff to prepare for the preemptive strike.

Captain Jellico's plan was to send a shuttle into the nebula and lay antimatter mines near the Cardassian ships. Once the mines were in place, the Cardassians would either have to meet his demands or be destroyed. Geordi informed Captain Jellico that placing the mines would be rather difficult and would require the best shuttle pilot available, Commander Riker.

So informed, Captain Jellico immediately went to Commander Riker's quarters. True to form, Captain Jellico minced no words. Setting aside their rank for the moment, Captain Jellico told Commander Riker that he neither liked him nor thought much of his leadership abilities. But as Mr. Riker was the best shuttle pilot on the ship, he was here to ask his help.

Commander Riker responded in kind. He told Captain Jellico that he didn't think much of him either. Will told Captain Jellico he was so arrogant and close-minded that he needed to control everything and everyone. He didn't provide an atmosphere of trust and didn't inspire the crew to go out of their way for him. Quite simply, Captain Jellico had everyone wound up so tight that there was no joy in anything. Furthermore, Will didn't think Jellico to be a particularly good captain.

But placing his duty to Starfleet and the *Enterprise* above his dislike of Captain Jellico, when asked—not ordered—to fly this dangerous mission, Commander Riker said he would pilot the shuttle.

After the mines were in place, Captain Jellico ordered a red alert and hailed Gul Lemec, who had returned to his own ship. Gul Lemec immediately protested that the *Enterprise* was in Cardassian territory, but he was interrupted by Captain Jellico, who told the Cardassian that he was not going to argue with him. Captain Jellico then informed Gul Lemec that every Cardassian ship inside the nebula was mined, he had his finger on the button, and Gul Lemec was in a very bad position. When the Cardassian said that he could not be intimidated, Captain Jellico detonated one of the mines—one placed too far from any ship to do any harm, but close enough to make the point. Indeed, it was a point well made, as Gul Lemec immediately asked Captain Jellico for his terms.

Captain Jellico demanded that the Cardassian ships leave the nebula one by one. Each ship was to eject its primary phaser coil before setting course for the nearest Cardassian base. I was also to be returned—immediately.

Despite being given orders to release me, Gul Madred continued his war of our wills. Gul Madred told me that the *Enterprise* had been hit and was burning in space and that the Cardassian invasion of Minos Korva had been successful. The Cardassians would tell the Federation that I had been killed during the invasion. Their intentions were to keep me prisoner for a very long, long time. I was devastated. But Gul Madred was willing to allow me to live out my life as a prisoner in comfort or pain—the choice was mine. All I needed to do was tell him how many lights I could see. Truthfully, I don't know what I would have said, but just then Gul Lemec entered the room, ordered Gul Madred to have me cleaned up, and immediately returned to the *Enterprise*. Before leaving him, I wanted to show Gul Madred that he had not broken my will. As such, I shouted at him, "There are four lights!"

After changing into my regular duty uniform and

filing my report with Starfleet, I went to the bridge, where Captain Jellico welcomed me back aboard the *Enterprise*. He reported that the *Enterprise* was just the way I had left her . . . maybe a little better. Then he directed the computer to transfer command back to me. That done, Captain Jellico departed for the *Cairo*.

I gave command of the bridge to Commander Riker and went to discuss the events of the past few days with Deanna.

Captain's personal journal: Observations on "Intellectual Honesty." Stardate 46422.3. En route to the Detrian System.

We are now under way to the Detrian System, where we hope to observe two gas-giant planets collide and thereby give birth to a new star. We are all very excited about the possibility to observe such an event, as watching a new star being created is not an experience many people are afforded in their lifetime. As I have some time available, I will now make my observations on the experience I reported on earlier for the purpose of illustrating the value of intellectual honesty.

Without question, being subjected to excruciating pain and torture at the hand of both the Borg and the Cardassians are two of the most debasing and painful experiences I have had during my many years of service in Starfleet. Regardless, I assure you that it is difficult for me to imagine a more humiliating experience for a starship captain to endure than being abruptly and rudely relieved of command, without cause or justification. For this reason, I cannot condone either why or how Admiral Nechayev relieved me of command of the *Enterprise* just to conduct one mission.

I also understand the necessity to take decisive action to protect and defend the interests of the Federation; however, this observation should not be taken to imply that every action taken in a crisis situation is always necessary. Quite frankly, I am at a loss to understand the thinking of senior officers who would send an away team on an extraordinarily dangerous mission without allowing them to be perfectly free to turn down the assignment.

Obviously, Admiral Nechayev placed great confidence in the ability of Captain Jellico to command the *Enterprise* during this mission. But I must be blunt in stating that this was an ill-considered action. Allow me to explain. Commander Riker had proven himself capable to command the *Enterprise* on several occasions. Moreover, the talks with the Cardassians could have been conducted by Captain Jellico aboard the *Enterprise* without being her captain. Quite simply, he could have remained in command of the *Cairo* and beamed aboard the *Enterprise* to conduct the talks. Moreover, if there was any reason to believe that the talks would fail and the Federation might have to take military action against the Cardassians, Captain Jellico was simply not the person to conduct such operations. Indeed, he had never been aboard a Galaxy-class starship, and there was no compelling reason to change command of the ship. Despite the fact that Captain Jellico had some experience in conducting peace talks with the Cardassians, his actions during this mission did not reflect those suited for diplomacy. Let there be no mistake, Captain Jellico's actions, as captain of the *Enterprise,* speak for themselves.

Despite the difficulties Admiral Nechayev and Captain Jellico created for members of my senior staff and the entire crew, I had every confidence that they would fulfill their duty to Starfleet and themselves. As our mission to Celtris III was one that perhaps required unusual security, clearly the mutual trust between Dr. Crusher, Worf, and me proved enough to hold us together during times of uncertainty.

Captain's personal journal: Lessons on "Intellectual Honesty." Stardate 46459.7. En route to a communication relay station near the Klingon border.

The *Enterprise* is presently in transit to a Federation communication relay station near the Klingon border, where we are scheduled to deliver supplies. I will use this period to record my lessons on intellectual honesty. As an officer you are entrusted to keep a high standard of personal honor; therefore, I submit these lessons for your consideration.

- Because humans are creatures of emotion, we can be drawn into doing the wrong thing by what, at the moment, seems a necessity— necessity that often proves to be the result of either ignorance or denial.

- I find that distrust arises in many ways. Indeed, an officer who gains some ends by selfish scheming and underhanded practice may imagine that he has found the key to success. But a day comes when he is understood and even his plausible words lose their value.

- One who is essentially dishonest is soon denied the chance to be honest because the doors of opportunity are closed to him. To be true to oneself is to be true to those who hold keys to the doors of opportunity.

- It is rather easy to recognize the faults of others, but it is much more difficult for one to admit that he may be responsible for the faults he finds in others.

- To be held in high regard, an officer's actions should not betray his words. Nevertheless, it is also vital that an officer's actions not betray doing what is right for the common good.

- An officer who is routinely true to himself and others is one who can be trusted and relied upon in a crisis situation. This is also true of other members of the crew.

- For reasons of security, an officer may not be able to fully disclose the nature of a mission to every member of the crew. Notwithstanding, under no circumstances should an officer ever mislead his crew as to the nature of the mission.

- There may be limited time for a new officer to begin developing a healthy relationship with his crew. But on no occasion should an officer use whatever limited time is available to undo the potential for a healthy relationship with the crew.

- The morale and motivation of the crew is a direct reflection of how they perceive their commander's integrity toward them.

Lastly,

- Intellectual honesty may result in one being dismissed for a time only to be recalled to duty when a mission's success depends upon one who can be trusted.

I am convinced that, as an officer in the Starfleet, one must not only act with integrity of word and deed, but of idea and principle. This should be nothing less than a Starfleet officer's code of honor. Make it so.

VIII

Interdependence

"Symbiosis"

Superintendent's foreword to "Interdependence."
*Advances in the design and construction of spacecraft
in the twenty-fourth century have virtually eliminated
the physical, mechanical, and technological defects
that posed hazards to earlier generations who ven-
tured into the final frontier. Nevertheless, in space,
neither survival nor mission success can be assured
by even the most advanced feats of engineers and
physicists.*

*For one and all, space is an unforgiving operating
environment. Travel among its interstellar bodies is
often dangerous and met with sudden, unpredictable
emergencies, which make for circumstances, conditions, and situations that can place both the Enterprise and its crew at risk. In addition, the mission of
the Enterprise cannot be achieved by one person
acting alone. Which explains why the crew of the*

Enterprise *mutually relied upon each other for both their safety and mission success.*

It is also important to understand that to those who serve Starfleet, interdependence neither begins nor ends aboard a spacecraft. Rather, interdependence within Starfleet begins everywhere and ends nowhere. As a leadership quality, being mutually dependent on others does not require an officer to abdicate rightful authority, to become complacent in executing duties, to relinquish individuality, or to think and act like the crowd to be accepted. Doing so would not only be wrong, it would either lead to chaos or result in Starfleet behaving like the Borg, whose principal vulnerability is found in their complete interdependence in which the "individual" is totally destroyed.

Interdependence is easy to talk about, difficult to enculturate, and can never be completely assured. Therefore, even in the twenty-fourth century, Starfleet must occasionally discipline officers whose ill-considered, independent actions place others at risk.

Admiral Andrea Brand
Superintendent, Starfleet Academy

Captain's personal journal: Stardate 44441.7. Departing Starbase 211.

Although the Federation has met many enemies in battle, diplomatic initiatives have led to peace treaties and armistices with some of the more hostile of our adversaries. Peace is often a fragile condition. Indeed, maintaining it requires every Starfleet officer to comply with the Federation's obligation to uphold its agreements with other peoples. For this reason, it is with a profound sense of disappointment that I report that a senior Starfleet officer recently jeopardized the Federation's peace with a former enemy. As this event illustrates, Starfleet officers who take ill-considered, independent action pose great danger to us all.

We were on a routine mapping survey near the Cardassian sector. It had been nearly a year since a peace treaty ended the long conflict between the Federation and Cardassia. Notwithstanding the treaty, the Cardassians remained nervous about protecting their border, which lies beyond Federation space, opposite from the Klingon and Romulan territories. For this reason, when Data reported the *Enterprise* to be nearing the boundary of Sector 21503, I told Mr. Worf to be on the lookout for a Cardassian patrol ship; one should be hailing us soon.

On the bridge, I reminisced with my staff about the last time I had been in this sector. While captain of the *U.S.S. Stargazer,* I had been sent on a mission to make preliminary overtures to a truce with the Cardassians. On first contact with the Cardassians, I lowered my shields as a gesture of goodwill. Indeed, my goodwill was lost on the Cardassians. They responded to my gesture by firing on my ship. They had taken out most of my weapons and damaged the impulse engine before I could regroup and run.

Commenting on this experience, Worf observed that the Cardassians had no honor and could not be trusted. Amused but not surprised by Worf's observation, Counselor Troi remarked that he had to trust the Cardassians now, they were our allies. True enough, but truer to his Klingon sense of honor, Worf reminded Deanna that trust must be earned, not given away.

I was anxious for the scout ship to contact us soon. Regardless of the peace treaty, it was not a good idea to remain along the Cardassian border too long without making your intentions known.

Shortly thereafter, and much to our total surprise, it was not a Cardassian scout ship that made contact with us. The *Enterprise* was unexpectedly rocked as we came under the attack of a Cardassian warship. As our red alert warning sounded, Worf detected that the Cardassians were preparing to fire again. I ordered him to increase power to our forward shields and hail the Cardassian ship. They didn't answer our hail and fired for the second time. Still unaware of what had provoked the Cardassian attack on our ship, I directed Worf to hail them again.

A damage report indicated that we had sustained minor damage before we put up our shields. Structural integrity was intact and we had sustained no casualties, but Commander La Forge reported that our starboard power coupling was down.

Ignoring our hails, the Cardassians continued their relentless attack on the *Enterprise.* I ordered evasive action and told Mr. Worf to ready our phasers. Directed to limit his fire to the Cardassian warship's shields and engines, Worf fired multiple phaser blasts. After taking several direct hits, the Cardassian warship was disabled and its captain stood down.

We hailed the Cardassian ship again. This time they answered our call. I identified myself, their captain identified himself as Gul Macet of the Cardassian ship *Trager.*

I asked Gul Macet why he had fired on us. He remarked that my question was curious: "In war, one attacks one's enemies."

Startled by his comment, I reminded the Cardassian that there was a treaty between our peoples. He said that perhaps that fact was unknown to the Federation starship that had destroyed one of their unarmed science stations two days ago. Now I was even more confused. I thought, Why would a Federation starship destroy a Cardassian space station? Such action would be a violation of our peace treaty and quite possibly start another war with the Cardassians.

I told Gul Macet that the Federation and the Cardassians had struggled too hard for peace to abandon it so easily. He reminded me that they were not the ones who had abandoned the peace. Then I told Gul Macet that I had no knowledge of this treaty violation and needed to talk to my superiors. As such, I requested that he give me an hour to find out what was behind these actions. The only alternative was for us to continue firing at one another. I advised the Cardassian captain that in such a contest he would be at a disadvantage, which might explain why he agreed to my request.

I proceeded to my ready room and hailed Admiral Haden, commander of Starfleet Security. After confirming my report, the admiral said that the Federation starship that attacked the Cardassian science station was the *U.S.S. Phoenix,* under the command of Captain Benjamin Maxwell.

This was shocking news. Ben Maxwell was one of Starfleet's finest captains. I observed to Admiral Haden that Captain Maxwell must surely have been provoked to take such action. Admiral Haden said that Starfleet wished they knew what happened. Captain Maxwell wouldn't respond to Starfleet's communiqués. Moreover, the *Phoenix* had gone on silent running.

Admiral Haden went on to inform me that the Cardassian science station the *Phoenix* had destroyed was in Sector 21505. Starfleet had no idea of the present whereabouts of the *Phoenix,* but suspected that she was still in Cardassian space.

I was ordered to go in and find the *Phoenix* and stop Captain Maxwell from causing further harm. Admiral Haden said the Cardassians had granted us safe passage for this mission. As a show of good faith, Starfleet had agreed to allow a small delegation of Cardassian observers to accompany us aboard the *Enterprise.* Without specifically referring to the Federation's recent encounter with the Borg, which resulted in the destruction of the greater part of our fleet, Admiral Haden reminded me that we were not prepared for a new, sustained conflict. As a consequence, the most important part of my mission was to preserve the peace, no matter what the cost.

Returning to the bridge, I briefed my senior staff on our new mission. Gul Macet and two aides would be transporting aboard the *Enterprise.* I had every intention of being open with them and allowing the Cardassians to join in our search for the *Phoenix*. Concerned with our ship's security, Mr. Worf wanted to guard the Cardassians while they were aboard the *Enterprise*. Respecting Worf's concerns, I told him they would be our guests and were not to be treated as prisoners. Nevertheless, I agreed to posting guards outside our ship's more sensitive areas, which would limit Cardassian access to them.

As a second precautionary measure, I instructed Counselor Troi to stay in close touch with the crew during this mission, as some of them might become uncomfortable with Cardassians on board. I didn't want there to be any incidents.

I then wondered aloud if anyone currently serving on the *Enterprise* had ever served with Captain Maxwell in previous assignments. Data reported that Chief O'Brien had served under Captain Maxwell's command aboard the *Rutledge*. I asked Commander Riker and Counselor Troi to greet our Cardassian guests in the transporter room, and, while there, inform Chief O'Brien that I would be paying him a visit.

We entered Cardassian territory and were unable to locate the *Phoenix*. Chief O'Brien joined members of my senior staff, the Cardassian observers, and me in the observation lounge to discuss the situation. Gul Macet was skeptical. He didn't believe that I was using every means at my disposal to track down one of the Federation's own starships.

I introduced Chief O'Brien to the Cardassian observers as someone who had previously served with Captain

Maxwell. Perhaps he could offer some insight as to why his former captain had taken such drastic, unauthorized action against the Cardassian science station.

Chief O'Brien told us that during the Cardassian war, Captain Maxwell's wife and children were killed during a raid on Setlik III. The Cardassians had mistaken this civilian outpost as a staging area from which the Federation was preparing to launch a massive attack and made a preemptive strike against it, killing nearly one hundred civilians in the process. Captain Maxwell was commanding the *U.S.S. Rutledge* at the time. The *Rutledge* arrived at Setlik III the morning after the raid—too late to save but a few people who lived in an outlying area.

Gul Macet surmised the death of Captain Maxwell's family to be the basis of his destruction of the Cardassian science station—it was an act of retribution for his own loss.

Just then, our meeting was interrupted by a call from Worf, who informed me that long-range sensors had located the *Phoenix*. I asked Gul Macet to join me on the bridge.

As we arrived, Mr. Data informed us that the *Phoenix* was in Sector 21505. We set a course to intercept. I also directed Mr. Worf to send a message ordering Captain Maxwell to prepare for a rendezvous with the *Enterprise*.

Gul Macet suggested that, since the Cardassians had a number of ships in Sector 21505, perhaps I should give him the *Phoenix*'s precise coordinates and its coded transponder frequency. So informed, the Cardassians could intercept the *Phoenix* far more quickly than could the *Enterprise.*

Fully aware of the urgent need to prevent Captain Maxwell from destroying any more Cardassian stations or spacecraft, I also understood that providing Gul Macet with the information he had requested would provide the Cardassians an opportunity to retaliate by destroying the *Phoenix.* Therefore, I chose to deny Gul Macet his request—at least for the time being. Under the circumstances, I preferred to be the one to make first contact with Captain Maxwell. And I didn't fully trust Gul Macet.

Closing on the *Phoenix,* we detected her to be pursuing a Cardassian supply ship. This surprised Gul Macet, as he had no previous knowledge of the Federation's capability to read Cardassian transponder codes —which allowed us to track their vessels. Indeed, Gul Macet wanted to know how we could do it, but I diverted his attention from our technology by reminding him that at the moment it was far more important that a Cardassian ship could be in jeopardy.

Mr. Worf informed me that the *Phoenix* had yet to answer our message. Captain Maxwell needed to understand that his refusal to answer our prior messages did not grant him impunity. So, I directed Worf to put out a repeating priority-one communiqué to the *Phoenix* on all subspace channels, "Break off your pursuit immediately!"

Gul Macet was becoming noticeably impatient with our efforts to stop the *Phoenix.* He asked me to show him the location of other Cardassian ships in the area. Seeing no danger in granting this request, I had Data display all Cardassian ships in the area on the computer screen. Making a quick study of the computer display, Gul Macet pointed out that one of their warships was closer to the *Phoenix* than we were. Then he said that, if I would just give him the Starfleet *Phoenix*'s transponder code the Cardassian warship could intercept Captain Maxwell before it was too late. By way of adding some drama to his request, the Cardassian asked if I was just going to stand idle and watch one of their ships be destroyed.

Once again, I asked Mr. Worf if the *Phoenix* had responded to *any* of our hails. He confirmed there had been no reply, which at the moment left me little choice. Fully aware that the greater part of my mission was to preserve the peace—whatever the cost—I ordered Mr. Worf to relay the *Phoenix*'s transponder code to the Cardassian warship. Mr. Worf protested my order as this classified information would give the Cardassians the ability to disable all of Starfleet's vessels. Fully understanding Worf's protest, I could not allow Captain Maxwell to destroy the Cardassian supply ship. However, I repeated my order, and, Mr. Worf complied without hesitation or protest.

Immediately after receiving our transmission, the Cardassian warship closed on the *Phoenix* and fired. The Cardassian fire damaged, but didn't disable, the *Phoenix*. Captain Maxwell took immediate evasive measures and moved his ship out of range of the Cardassian warship's weapons before returning fire. On the computer screen we witnessed the *Phoenix*'s photon torpedoes destroy the Cardassian warship.

Captain Maxwell's latest action was very disturbing to all of us. The combined Cardassian casualties of Captain Maxwell's continuing assault came to 650 lives—the warship carried a crew of six hundred, the supply ship, fifty. There could be no further delay. Captain Maxwell had to be stopped, which meant we had to intercept the *Phoenix* as soon as possible!

At our present speed of warp four, Mr. Data informed me that it would take sixteen hours forty-four minutes to intercept the *Phoenix*. I ordered our speed increased to warp nine.

I left the bridge and went to speak with Chief O'Brien. I asked him, based on his previous experience with Captain Maxwell, "What has gone wrong?"

The chief said there was a reason for what Captain Maxwell was doing—those Cardassians were up to something. "They had to be."

Chief O'Brien went on to say that despite the fact that Cardassians had killed his entire family his former captain was not a man given to retaliation. The Cardassians had to be the ones who were up to something—I should be investigating them, not Captain Maxwell.

I returned to the bridge and had no sooner arrived than Worf entered with one of the Cardassian observers in hand. Over the Cardassian's protest of innocence, Worf said he had caught him at a computer station trying to access information on the *Enterprise*'s weapons systems. The Cardassian said that he had been studying the terminal's interface systems, which were more advanced than those on his own ship—he had no idea what was in the files.

Gul Macet appeared upset by his subordinate's actions. Without further questioning, Gul Macet ordered this aide returned to his quarters, where he was to remain confined. Privately, Gul Macet told me that he was very disappointed with his aide's action and would discipline him once they had returned to their own ship. I considered the matter closed and told the Cardassian captain he was free to take whatever action he deemed appropriate. He thanked me for my generosity in the matter. After which, I commented that if the peace between our two peoples was to last, we could not allow the actions of any one man to come between us. Gul Macet agreed. Then he said that although there were those who desired war, he was not one of them, and could see by my actions that neither was I.

Perhaps as we had yet to stop the *Phoenix,* it was not an appropriate time to say so, but I believed Worf's report to be a correct one. Moreover, in light of their earlier questions about our sensors, I found myself becoming rather distrustful of the Cardassian observers. However, for the time being I kept my suspicions to myself.

We continued our intercept course and closed on the *Phoenix,* and established communications with Captain Maxwell. He agreed to meet me aboard the *Enterprise.*

Commander Riker proceeded to the transporter

room, where Chief O'Brien was on duty, to welcome Captain Maxwell aboard. Surprised and pleased to see Mr. O'Brien, Maxwell told Commander Riker that Chief O'Brien was the finest tactical officer that had ever served under his command.

In my ready room, Mr. Riker introduced Captain Maxwell to me. Although we had not previously met, I was well aware of his outstanding record. Captain Maxwell remarked that I must be thinking that he had gone completely mad. Frankly, the thought had occurred to me.

Captain Maxwell said that he was relieved when he learned I was the one the Federation had sent to find him. He believed me to be someone who knew what was really going on in this sector; therefore, I would be able to understand what he had been doing. It came as somewhat of a surprise to Captain Maxwell when I told him that I knew of nothing that could possibly justify what he had done.

Captain Maxwell said that the Cardassians were rearming. Their so-called science station was nothing more than a staging area that would serve as a jumping-off point into three Federation sectors. The supply ships were not carrying scientific equipment, but were secretly transporting matériel to the science station. He could show me no documentation to support his claim, but insisted it was an accurate one—he knew what the Cardassians were doing.

I asked him why he had not informed Starfleet of his findings. Captain Maxwell said those at Starfleet Command were just too slow, too bureaucratic, to act before the Cardassians completed their preparations. He had no faith that Starfleet Command had a clue as to what was really going on out in this sector. Apparently, he believed as *he* knew what the Cardassians were up to, *he* was justified in taking unauthorized action to stop them before it was too late—lives were at stake, *he* had to act.

Captain Maxwell went on to tell me that he believed the Cardassians had entered the peace treaty as a ruse to give them time to rebuild their forces. He also firmly believed that his initiatives against the Cardassians were going to prevent a new war.

I couldn't have agreed less. The *Phoenix* had not been threatened. And if his suspicions were true, it was not his place to take decisions that were rightly those of higher authority at Starfleet Command.

I told Captain Maxwell that I believed him—an outstanding officer with a superior service record—to have abandoned the very fundamental principles that he had believed in and even fought for all of his life. The point of my observation was to inform Captain Maxwell that I believed his actions to be ones to avenge the death of his wife and children.

Captain Maxwell protested, denying my allegations and adding me to his list of Starfleet fools. Nevertheless, the captain wanted me to go with him and find a Cardassian supply ship—its cargo would provide evidence to support his claims.

I told Captain Maxwell that we were not going after any more Cardassian supply ships. He was going to return to his ship and set a course for Starbase 211.

Starfleet had given me orders to have the *Phoenix* and the *Enterprise* return to Federation space together. Then, rather bluntly, I advised him that I would allow him the dignity of retaining command of his ship on our voyage to Starbase 211. But if he refused to follow my orders, I would throw him in the *Enterprise*'s brig and tow the *Phoenix* back in disgrace. Considering his options, Captain Maxwell agreed to follow my orders. Reflecting back on the situation, I should not have trusted Captain Maxwell to keep his word. After all, he had been committing acts more serious than disobeying orders.

Under way to Starbase 211, we followed the *Phoenix* in close formation. Before long, however, the *Phoenix* abruptly changed course and gave chase after a Cardassian supply ship. We immediately changed course and pursued. As we tracked his ship, Captain Maxwell would not answer our hails. Although I didn't relish the idea of having to employ them against a Federation starship, I ordered Mr. Worf to arm our phasers.

After stopping the Cardassian vessel, Captain Maxwell hailed me. On the screen, he said that if I needed proof that the Cardassians were rearming, I had it now. The evidence was on the supply ship.

Disregarding the Cardassian vessel, I sternly advised Captain Maxwell that he had disobeyed a direct order. Obviously, he had no intentions of following my orders. I informed Captain Maxwell that the Cardassian vessel would not be boarded. He was to beam aboard the *Enterprise.*

Disregarding my new order, Captain Maxwell said that if I would not board the Cardassian ship, he would destroy it. The situation was critical, but I was not about to waver. I assure you that I had every intention of carrying out my duty to preserve the peace, even if it meant that I had to destroy the *Phoenix*. To that end, I informed Captain Maxwell that I would use every means at my disposal to see that he did not destroy the Cardassian vessel.

Just then, Chief O'Brien came to the bridge to provide us with his insights on what actions his former captain might take under the present circumstances. O'Brien suggested that Captain Maxwell would strike if he felt he had his back against a wall. At the same time we saw that the *Phoenix* had raised her shields and was arming weapons. Captain Maxwell left me with no option. I ordered a red alert and our weapons readied. It now appeared as if I was going to have to attack the *Phoenix* in order to preserve the peace.

As we prepared to fire, Chief O'Brien interjected and requested my permission to beam aboard the *Phoenix* and to talk to his former captain. Chief O'Brien believed he knew Captain Maxwell well enough to get him to cooperate. His request posed a new problem. The *Phoenix*'s shields were raised and no one could transport through them. Notwithstanding, Chief O'Brien said he understood the *Phoenix* to have a one-fiftieth-of-a-second window in the high-energy wave cycles used to power her shields. This window was just enough time for him to transport to the *Phoenix*.

As I didn't relish the idea of destroying a Federation

starship or its crew, I granted Chief O'Brien his request. Nevertheless, if his mission proved unsuccessful, the situation wouldn't be any more precarious than it was already. I don't know what occurred in the conversation between Chief O'Brien and his former captain, but Chief O'Brien convinced Captain Maxwell to turn command of the *Phoenix* over to his first officer and return to the *Enterprise.*

We soon resumed our course to Starbase 211. Much to my relief, the peace had been preserved.

Captain's personal journal: Observations on "Interdependence." Stardate 44452.4 En route to Sector 21503.

After escorting the *Phoenix* and Captain Maxwell to Starbase 211, and making a full report of our mission, the *Enterprise* is returning to Sector 21503, where we will resume our mapping survey. En route, I will record my observations on recent events as they relate to the leadership quality of interdependence.

To be sure, there are many lessons that can be drawn from our mission to stop Captain Maxwell and maintain peace with the Cardassians. One of these is can be found in the events that took place in the observation lounge as this mission came to a close.

As soon as Chief O'Brien and he returned to the *Enterprise,* I confined Captain Maxwell to his quarters until we reached Starbase 211. I then called Mr. O'Brien to the observation lounge—where Gul Macet and I were meeting for the last time—and thanked the chief for taking the initiative to help bring the situation to a successful conclusion.

After Mr. O'Brien left the lounge, the Cardassian captain remarked that O'Brien's loyalty to Captain Maxwell was admirable, if not misplaced. I told him that the loyalty that he would so lightly dismiss had not come easily to people of the Federation. Apparently, the Cardassians still had much to learn about us. I went on to inform Gul Macet that Captain Maxwell had earned the loyalty and trust of his crew. In war, Captain Maxwell was twice honored with the Federation's highest citation for courage and valor. Moreover, I said that if he could not find a role for himself in peace, we could pity Captain Maxwell, but we could not dismiss him.

What Gul Macet failed to understand is that within the Federation, loyalty and trust are not taken for granted. An officer must earn the loyalty and trust of those under his command. Once earned, these qualities are not quickly abandoned. Indeed, Starfleet officers very often have to help those under their command through difficult times. As such, an officer's crew will stand by him in his time of need.

Another lesson can be found in the behavior of the Cardassian observers while on board the *Enterprise*. Our orders were to allow the Cardassians to assist us in stopping Captain Maxwell. Although we took some security precautions, the Cardassians were treated as our partners in this effort. Regardless, their attempts at espionage clearly violated both the trust we extended to them as well as the treaty between our two peoples.

I recognized that the Cardassians' behavior had been

less than honorable while on my ship and came to understand why. For this reason, I felt it important to give Gul Macet an important message to take back to his leaders.

As he started to leave, I told the Cardassian that there was one more thing I had to say to him. Captain Maxwell had been right. The Cardassians were rearming for war. But as I was there to preserve the peace, I did not attempt to board the Cardassian supply ship. If I had made such an attempt, the peace would have been lost. That said, I told Gul Macet to tell his leaders that we would be watching.

I believe that my account of this event provides clear illustration of the interdependence among my crew. However, it was perhaps Chief O'Brien's individual initiative that was the pivotal factor that turned a potentially bad situation into a successful mission. We were fortunate to have Chief O'Brien serving aboard the *Enterprise* at the time.

Captain's personal journal: Lessons on "Interdependence." Stardate 44472.2. En route to Ventax II.

The *Enterprise* has just been ordered by Starfleet to respond to an emergency transmission from the director of the Federation science station on Ventax II. Apparently, widespread panic has set in among the people there in anticipation of the arrival of Ardra, a legendary supernatural being. Although I am rather curious about what awaits us at Ventax II, I will use some of our transit time to record my lessons on interdependence.

To be sure, interdependence can be either a great strength or a fatal weakness. If interdependence is to be a quality that will strengthen your leadership, you must always allow the *individual* to strive within an environment of mutual dependence. If not, the loss of the *individual* will surely become a fatal weakness—an Achilles' heel—as it has for the Borg.

To the end that you will employ interdependence as a quality that strengthens your leadership, I offer the following lessons.

- Whenever a distinguished officer suddenly behaves in an erratic way, one which is contrary to both his past record and the well-being of the Federation, there is usually misguided rationalization for it. Yet, as they have served the Federation in its hour of need, it is noble to help them work through their personal crisis.
- Knowledge is power. But, withholding information from those with whom it should be rightfully shared is a personal weakness, one for which others often pay a heavy price.
- It is every officer's duty to freely exchange his knowledge, not by way of expressing intellectual superiority, but as a means by which one helps others solve problems and improve decisions.
- On becoming a senior officer, one does not gain the authority to act independent of either Federation policy or Starfleet general order. Rather,

senior officers should be duty-bound to abide by the policies and orders of higher command as they set the example others imitate.

- Every member of the crew has the right and duty to make meaningful contributions to the mission of their starship. However, no one has the right to use Federation resources to pursue a personal agenda.

- Great care should be taken to preserve the "individual" that exists in all who serve under your command. Quite frankly, one's individualism—found in specialized abilities and knowledge—is a key asset that contributes to achieving common good for all.

- An officer who asks for the help of others, that he might accomplish a task or succeed at his mission, is not weak, but wise. An officer who provides help to others is not an intruder, but a friend.

- There are times when virtually every officer will become skeptical of those in higher positions. However, one's skepticism of senior officers neither justifies withholding information nor condones taking independent action.

- Sometimes the behavior of great officers crosses over the line of propriety and must be reigned in by a strong commander.

- Starfleet Command has every right to expect that all officers will make good on their oath of office. In other words, officers of the Starfleet are to be reliable, dependable, trustworthy, and

mutually supportive. Surely, the very moment an officer abdicates his oath of office he loses his value to Starfleet.

And by way of concluding these lessons on interdependence,

- One good officer sometimes makes the difference in the success or failure of a mission. The truth is, however, the cooperative, collaborative, and corroborative effort of the entire crew is much more likely to result in mission success.

Make no mistake about it, as a Starfleet officer you will never have a more satisfying assignment than when serving among others with whom you share mutual dependence . . . an interconnection . . . even a symbiotic relationship. Make it so.

IX

Resilience

"Mortality Fail-Safe"

Superintendent's foreword to "Resilience." *Deep-space travel affects the physical conditioning and psychological health of even the most physically fit and well-adjusted travelers. Therefore, the Enterprise-D was equipped with twenty-four holographic environment simulators, commonly called "holodecks," which provided members of the crew and their families an opportunity to stimulate their minds and exercise their bodies in ways not otherwise available to them on a spacecraft. Located on Deck 11, the four main holodecks were large enough to accommodate small group activities. Individual activity was provided in any of the twenty personal holographic environment simulators located on Decks 12 and 33.*

The holodeck used two main computer subsystems, the holographic imagery subsystem and the matter-conversion subsystem, to create remarkably sophisticated simulation programs. The integration of these subsystems allowed for the creation of high-fidelity simulations containing image, sound, and tactile qualities that are virtually indistinguishable from reality. Holodeck computers had a library containing a variety of preprogrammed recreation, sports, and training simulations. These preprogrammed simulations could be customized to either personal or group specifications.

New software was installed in the Enterprise-D's holodeck systems in 2364 by the Bynars at Starbase 74. This upgrade allowed holodeck users to create simulated versions of real persons by making use of file photos, voice recordings, and personality profile databases. It also provided for interactive behavior between simulated persons and holodeck participants based on the actions of users. However, the use of these new features without the prior consent of the persons being simulated was a serious invasion of privacy and breach of holodeck etiquette.

Because holodeck participants could—knowingly or unknowingly—be subjected to physical danger, sensors were installed to prevent serious injury to users. A subroutine of the Enterprise's holodeck control programs that provided this safeguard was known as the mortality fail-safe. Under normal operating conditions, the mortality fail-safe stopped a holodeck program in progress upon detecting immediate serious danger to users or when a user gave it a voice command to do so. When functioning as intended, the mortality fail-safe permitted holodeck users to push the limits of any holodeck situation without concern for their physical safety.

On occasion, however, the mortality fail-safe subroutine was overridden or otherwise disabled. It could also be overridden by the voice command of two senior officers. Under any of these low-probability conditions, holodeck users could be placed in potentially danger-

*ous situations, and the only safeguard against seri-
ous injury, or even death, was their judgment and
skill.*

Admiral Andrea Brand
Superintendent, Starfleet Academy

Captain's personal Journal: Stardate 42931.6. Departing the Braslota System.

Aboard a starship, one must always be prepared for the unexpected. To be sure, the adventure and danger we have experienced over the past few days were quite unexpected. I now find myself thoroughly relieved to have just officially ended our first battle simulation. Although Starfleet Command intended this simulation as preparation for the looming Borg threat, the exercise turned into an empirical test of our combat-readiness when the Ferengi interrupted the war games.

As the *Enterprise*'s primary purpose is exploration, I had initial misgivings over Starfleet's request to divert to the Braslota System to be part of a military exercise. Apart from my skepticism, I was keenly aware of the Borg threat and knew that my crew and I needed to hone our tactical skills. Serving as Starfleet's observer and mediator for this exercise was a Zakdorn master strategist, Sirna Kolrami.

Prior to events that would take place during this war-game exercise, the Zakdorn reputation had not been challenged by potential foes in actual conflict for over nine millennia. However, the Zakdorn are a humanoid race long considered as having the most innately superior strategic minds in the universe. They are also known for their posture of arrogance, imperious self-confidence, and strutting self-assurance.

The plans for this war-game exercise called for us to proceed to the second planet in the Braslota System, where the *U.S.S. Hathaway,* a derelict, out-of-service, eighty-year-old Federation starcruiser was in orbit. A complement of forty from our own crew would act as the opposing force for this exercise. After being beamed aboard the *Hathaway,* they would be given forty-eight hours to revive her and prepare for an attack by the *Enterprise.* In order to present the exercise as realistically as possible, the *Enterprise*'s weapons would be disconnected and interlinked with modified laser pulse beams. The *Hathaway*'s weapons had already been removed and her systems modified to simulate combat. All hits would be recorded electronically, and registered damage would cause the main computer to shut down the affected areas for the appropriate repair time. Master Kolrami was present to evaluate the combat-readiness of both the *Enterprise* and our crew.

I appointed Commander Riker as captain of the *Hathaway* for this exercise and told him he was free to choose his complement of forty from among our crew, excepting Mr. Data, who would serve as my Number One during the battle simulation. However, Master Kolrami questioned my decision to place Mr. Riker in command of the *Hathaway* and suggested that I select the crews for both ships. Despite Mr. Kolrami's reservation, Mr. Riker was the right choice to command the opposing ship for this exercise, and I didn't have to justify this choice to anyone. Moreover, I informed Mr. Kolrami that aboard the *Enterprise,* the leader of the away team has full control of the mission, which includes the right to select its members.

Commander Riker choose well indeed. Among others, he selected Lieutenant La Forge and Lieutenant Junior Grade Worf to serve with him aboard the *Hathaway.* I also granted Mr. Riker my permission to have Acting Ensign Wesley Crusher join his crew as an observer. Commander Riker thought serving on the *Hathaway* during this exercise would provide Wesley with some valuable practical experience before he departed to Starfleet Academy. I agreed.

During our three-day transit to the Braslota System, Commander Riker invited Mr. Kolrami to join him in a game of *strategema.* A third-level grand master of strategema, Sirna Kolrami is simply the best player of this game in the Federation. He considered Mr. Riker's invitation audacious but agreed to play after commenting that it can often be quite diverting to play an opponent of limited dimensions. Commander Riker had no misconceptions about his ability to defeat Master Kolrami, but simply considered it a privilege to play him.

Master Kolrami won the match soon after it began, which came with some disappointment to the crew. They had hoped, and even bet, that Commander Riker would at least play a competitive game. The dismissive air and flippant flamboyance Mr. Kolrami exhibited, after his all too easy victory, motivated Dr. Pulaski, who was the Enterprise's chief medical officer during the year Beverly spent serving as chief of Starfleet Medical, to find a way to deflate the Zakdorn's offending ego.

Meanwhile, Commander Riker and his crew had beamed aboard the *Hathaway* to ready her for the exercise. Finding the ship in worse condition than expected, Mr. Riker hailed me to voice his concern over the gross mismatch between the *Hathaway* and the *Enterprise*. He was outequipped, outgunned, and outmanned. How could we expect him to put up much of a fight? A valid point, but one to which Mr. Kolrami curtly remarked that the Zakdorn don't fret over the inequalities in life, but thrive on challenge. Mr. Kolrami then informed Commander Riker that how he performed in a mismatch was precisely the interest Starfleet had in this mission.

I resented these and other denigrating and abusive comments Sirna Kolrami had made toward Mr. Riker. Therefore, I asked Mr. Kolrami to meet with me in my ready room, where I demanded to know the root of his prejudice toward Commander Riker. Mr. Kolrami informed me that in reviewing Commander Riker's record he found flaws in the jocular manner in which Mr. Riker conducted himself on occasion. Mr. Kolrami then added a personal observation to the effect that leaders are born, not made. Indeed, a flawed notion with no basis in fact. I advised Mr. Kolrami that he was confusing style with intent. Further, I told him, the test of a leader is whether the crew will follow where he leads, and it was Commander Riker's style that instilled loyalty in the crew to follow his lead. I also informed Mr. Kolrami that Commander Riker was simply the finest officer I had ever known. The source of his prejudice revealed and my confidence in Commander Riker made clear, we returned to the bridge.

While "Captain" Riker and his crew continued preparations for the impending battle simulation, Dr. Pulaski deftly maneuvered Data and Mr. Kolrami into playing a game of strategema—a match of man against machine. On accepting this challenge, Kolrami remarked to Data that he would be playing for the reputation of the *Enterprise.* Obviously this was a remark Mr. Kolrami intended to place pressure on his opponent, but it was also one to which our good doctor added greater pressure by telling Data that his own reputation would be on the line. Anxious to see Data beat the confident Kolrami, several of the crew assembled to watch the match. However, such an outcome was not to be; the Zakdorn proved too skillful at strategema for even the most sophisticated machine in the galaxy. Master Kolrami was obviously pleased with his victory, and Data took his defeat very hard.

Returning to his quarters to perform diagnostic checks of his computer systems, Commander Data temporarily removed himself from duty on the bridge. Counselor Troi and our chief medical officer Dr. Pulaski tried to tell Data that there was nothing wrong with him, losing is a normal part of life. Data interpreted their counsel as applicable to humanoid life-forms, not androids. In losing, Data deduced that he had proven to be deficient in some way. Until he found and corrected the apparent malfunction in his circuits, he would not return to the bridge, because at the moment his judgment was suspect.

Shortly before the battle simulation was scheduled to begin, Dr. Pulaski and Counselor Troi informed me that Data was suffering from a profound loss of confidence. Only I could restore his balance. I was truly puzzled. How could Data, a machine, be suffering from a human condition? Dr. Pulaski suggested that whether caused by human emotion or android algorithms, the effects were still the same. Consequently, Data was not on the bridge and wouldn't return until we found some way to address his problems. Thus, less than one hour away from a battle simulation, I had to restore the confidence of an android who was acting as my Number One for the exercise.

I quickly made my way to Data's quarters and reminded him that I required his presence on the bridge. Data politely told me that I would be better served by selecting another to be my first officer for the time being. Although he had made no mistakes during the stratagema match and could detect no malfunction in his circuitry, he was in the process of making further checks with the ship's main computer. Data said that I would be ill-advised to rely on his judgment until the problem had been located and fixed. He had proven fallible and might make a mistake as he had not been able to isolate the problem.

To say the least, I was irritated by Data's reluctance to perform his duties. As such, I rather sternly informed Commander Data that yes, he might make a mistake, but that did not alter his duty to me and to the

Enterprise. I then asked if he could formulate a premise. He affirmed that he could. I then told him to formulate how to deal with Commander Riker and the *Hathaway* and that I would await his answer on the bridge. I further observed to Data that it is possible to commit no mistakes and still lose; that is not a weakness, it is life. As I stepped through the doorway, I turned to Mr. Data and firmly told him to leave his hesitation and self-doubt in his quarters. So advised, Mr. Data was quickly rededicated to his duties.

Meanwhile, back on the *Hathaway,* Worf had used his knowledge of the *Enterprise*'s security override to devise a way to display false holographic images—illusions—on our main viewscreen. Concurrently, Ensign Crusher had gained permission to return to the *Enterprise* using the ruse that he needed to tend to an experiment he had left running. As we later found out, Wesley's real purpose was to obtain some antimatter necessary to restore the *Hathaway*'s warp-drive capability, if only for a few seconds.

Forty-eight hours had passed since Commander Riker and his crew beamed aboard the *Hathaway.* Now, with both spacecraft prepared for battle simulation, Mr. Kolrami ordered the war games to begin. As we maneuvered the *Enterprise* into her first attack position, a Romulan warship unexpectedly appeared on our main screen. We were taken by surprise and thought this image to be real. However, it was an illusion. Mr. Riker and his crew took advantage of our momentary confusion and fired on the *Enterprise.* The *Hathaway* had struck the first blow in our war-game exercise, and our computers responded as if this blow came from actual phaser fire. Our tactical officer estimated that it would take three point six days to repair the simulated damage to the *Enterprise.* I now realized the Romulan ship had been nothing more than an illusion, one that Mr. Worf had used his knowledge of the *Enterprise*'s security codes to create. To prevent us from being duped a second time, I ordered Mr. Data to input new sensor codes—ones that Worf could not override.

As the *Enterprise* came about to launch a counterattack on the *Hathaway,* we were met with yet another surprise. Out of nowhere, a Ferengi warship suddenly appeared on our viewscreen. Thinking I hadn't given Mr. Worf enough credit, I believed he must have found a way to defeat Data's new sensor codes. Quite frankly, I took the Ferengi warship to be another illusion. As I was to soon find out, however, I was mistaken. The Ferengi warship fired on the *Enterprise,* and our ship sustained physical damage.

Under normal conditions, we would have detected this oncoming intruder long before it could have fired upon us. However, with our sensors and weapons reconfigured for the battle simulation, we were an easy target, and not immediately able to defend ourselves. As the Ferengi fire also disabled our transporters, Commander Riker and his crew were trapped on board the *Hathaway* without a way to defend themselves.

Attempting to invoke his authority as Starfleet's observer for this battle simulation, which had suddenly become a crisis situation, Kolrami ordered me to retreat. According to his theoretical way of viewing war, sacrificing Commander Riker and his crew of forty to save the *Enterprise* and its contingent of one thousand was an acceptable battle loss under the circumstances. Perhaps his rationale for our retreat could be supported in theory, but this was not a laboratory and I found retreat totally unacceptable. Without giving his presumptive orders a second thought, I informed Mr. Kolrami that I was the captain of the *Enterprise* and I was not about to retreat.

Hailing the Ferengi vessel, I identified myself and demanded the reason for their attack. The Ferengi identified himself as Bractor, captain of the *Kreechta.* Mistakenly, they had assumed our battle simulation to an actual encounter in progress. They could not understand why the *Enterprise* would be attacking another Federation vessel, especially one their sensors showed as having no weapons and only a skeleton crew; unless, of course, the Ferengi surmised, this vessel contained something of great value to the *Enterprise.* True to their reputation as a race enculturated with extraordinary greed, the Ferengi interest was in securing this thing of value for themselves. They were also curious as to why we had not taken defensive action on their approach. Fully aware that the *Enterprise* was crippled, Bractor positioned the *Kreechta* to fire on us. The Ferengi then demanded I surrender the *Hathaway* to them and they would allow the *Enterprise* to leave unharmed. Bractor gave me ten minutes to comply with his terms or he would launch an attack.

Due to a miscalculation on my part, the *Enterprise*

had been subjected to this surprise attack. While Mr. Kolrami repeated his call for our retreat, I had no intention of abandoning Commander Riker and his crew. My actions had caused them to be stranded aboard a derelict starship with no ability to defend themselves, and I was resolved to find a way to protect them as well as the *Enterprise.*

I immediately met with my senior officers to seek their suggestions. Commander Riker had been monitoring the situation from his position aboard the *Hathaway* and joined in our discussion on the viewscreen. Data reasoned that the Ferengi perceived the *Hathaway* to be something of great value and that we must remove it from their field of interest. On learning from Commander Riker that the *Hathaway* now had a limited warp-drive capability, and with some of our weapons brought back to normal operating conditions, Data suggested we fire four photon torpedoes at the *Hathaway*. One millisecond after detonation, Geordi would engage the warp drive and the *Hathaway* would accelerate beyond harm's way. From the Ferengi point of view, this illusory tactic would make it appear as if we had destroyed their prize.

It was a grand strategy indeed, but as the *Hathaway*'s restored warp-drive capability had not been tested, it could prove deadly for everyone aboard. I could not order Commander Riker to go along. Fully aware of the risks involved, Will agreed to our plan and commented, "What the hell. No one ever said life was safe."

I returned to the bridge and hailed the Ferengi ship. I informed them that their actions had been wholly criminal and they would not profit by them—I would deny them their prize. That said, we fired away.

Much to our good fortune, everything went according to plan. Indeed, from the Ferengi ship's perspective it appeared as though we had destroyed the *Hathaway*. Enraged by the apparent loss of his prize, Bractor was preparing to fire on us when another Federation starship suddenly appeared on the *Kreechta*'s sensors. Mistakenly believing that he had been outmaneuvered, Bractor ordered a retreat. However, the approaching vessel was simply another holographic illusion created by our Mr. Worf.

The *Enterprise*'s transporters were quickly repaired, and with Commander Riker and his away team now safely back on board, I officially concluded the battle simulation and we set course for the nearest starbase.

Despite the Zakdorn's reputation, he had been no use to us in battle. Perhaps this explains why Master Kolrami appeared somewhat contrite when he told me that he had no choice but to agree with my earlier assessment of Commander Riker. Mr. Kolrami then added that we had all performed our duties well . . . his report to Starfleet would be most favorable.

Under way, Mr. Data accepted the Grand Master's offer of a rematch at strategema. This time, Data was prepared. They began a game that was to last longer than any other in the history of strategema. A bewildered Kolrami soon realized he could not win and in a fit of frustration, he abruptly quit. In the strictest sense, the match ended in a stalemate. Despite this technicality, the crew took the tie as a clear victory for Data, who had truly defeated the Zakdorn and his ego.

Quite simply, Data had altered his premise for this match. Knowing that Master Kolrami would play to win and expect him to do the same, Data had played for a draw, which proved to be a fine premise indeed.

Captain's personal journal: Observations on "Resilience." Stardate 42941.5. At Starbase 365.

The most important leadership lessons that can be drawn from our first battle simulation are found in the varying degrees of personal and crew resilience that surfaced in the face of both challenge and danger. I assure you that, from oversights to blunders, the errors made during the mission clearly substantiate my conviction that no officer, no expert, and no technology is infallible. As confirmed by the ultimate success of this experience in the Braslota System, it is also my strongly held belief that fallibility is neither incapacitating nor insurmountable.

Sirna Kolrami soiled much of the Zakdorn and his own reputation in but two moments of ill-considered action. Confronted by a real—not theoretical—hostile force, Kolrami's strategy was one of self-preservation at the sacrifice of others. Perhaps Master Kolrami could successfully defend this strategy before an audience of inexperienced cadets at the Academy, but aboard the *Enterprise* ordering me to retreat was taken as a sign of weakness, if not cowardice. Mr. Kolrami dealt a second blow to his reputation when he abruptly withdrew from his strategema rematch with Data. Rather than risking his undefeated streak, the Zakdorn master opted to stop a match that he could not win and might lose. Despite Mr. Kolrami's justifications for his withdrawal, in the minds of the *Enterprise*'s crew the haughty Zakdorn was justly beaten in a game of strategy and will. As Mr. Kolrami remains a Starfleet strategist, I can only hope that his pride and vanity will soon allow him to learn how to properly deal with crisis situations, mistakes, and misfortunes.

Despite Sirna Kolrami's disparaging and snide remarks concerning Mr. Riker's leadership ability, there was never any doubt in my mind that my Number One would retain his cheerfulness and courage throughout every phase of this mission. Commander Riker's adventurous nature was evidenced in his challenging Master Kolrami in strategema, a match Will knew he would not win. As captain of the *Hathaway,* Mr. Riker employed a masterful tactic that landed the first blow in simulated combat against a far superior spacecraft, the *Enterprise.* Facing impending disaster, if not the possibility of death, Commander Riker had the courage to place his fate, and that of his crew, in the hands of trusted shipmates. Bold and risky, this decision was essential to our ability to remove the Ferengi threat.

Commander Data's reluctance to perform his official duties after losing a simple game of strategema was quite unexpected. The basic truth is that even the most advanced technology can, at times, be unreliable. Still, Data could not accept the possibility that his programming would allow him to err, which created a problem that required my intervention. Once Data understood that I would accept the possibility that he might make a mistake, but that I was unwilling to put up with his self-doubt and hesitation, he quickly recovered and was back to attending to his duties as my Number One for the battle simulation. Later, we witnessed that Data learned from his experience with fallibility.

Lieutenant Worf, Ensign Crusher, and Lieutenant La Forge's resilience was manifest in their improvising methods and tactics to overcome what to some people would be indomitable odds. Without question, they lived up to the expectations Commander Riker had for them when he asked them to join him on the *Hathaway*.

As for my own miscalculations, they placed the *Enterprise* and her crew in great jeopardy. Indeed, even though I ordered long-range scans of the Braslota System prior to the start of the war games, it was a mistake not to keep a portion of our sensors and weapons systems on-line during the battle simulation. Simply put, there is no secure place in deep space, yet I did not act accordingly. We should have retained a portion of the *Enterprise*'s defensive and offensive capabilities during the simulation. Had we done so, the *Kreechta* would have been detected before it could fire on us.

I must also comment on the Ferengi. Bractor and his crew were seeking something they perceived to be of great value. When denied their prize, the Ferengi marauders were enraged and sought revenge against a disabled *Enterprise.* However, without the certainty of victory, the Ferengi apparently lacked the nerve to carry out their criminal intentions, which was quite acceptable to me.

Captain's personal journal: Lessons on "Resilience." Stardate 42968.3. En route to Surata IV.

As a Starfleet officer, you are expected to be of resilient character; therefore, developing and maintaining this quality will be one of your top priorities. It is also your responsibility to nurture the experiences of those under your command to help them develop a sense of competence and self-confidence for dealing with and overcoming their misfortunes and mistakes. You must recognize that, at any level of command, an officer must take steps to insure his own resilience and the stability and strength of his unit. To these ends, the following lessons on resilience are offered for your consideration.

- I assure you that the first step in forging either personal or crew resilience is taken when an officer begins to place his trust in others.
- By confiding in others, an officer takes two important steps toward building resilience in them. By sharing experiences verbally, you integrate emotionally and bond a sense of mortal trust with them.
- Allowing those under your command to have a great deal of control over how they accomplish

assignments reinforces your confidence in them. It also motivates their desire to perform their duties well.

- It is prudent that you be driven to serve purposes outside your own self-interest, as the extreme individualist never succeeds as an officer.

- A Starfleet officer is to forgive and forget the honest errors of others and help them rebound from their mistakes. This is a paramount responsibility.

- It is vital that you do not become confounded by your miscalculations when a particular strategy is not working. In light of such a situation, your task is to formulate a new premise and take decisive action.

- In matters of either crisis or routine, it is always wise to ask for the ideas, opinions, or suggestions of others. Indeed, this practice often improves action taken and reinforces consensus between an officer and those he commands. Moreover, I believe that restricting your choices to the confines of your own knowledge is self-limiting. This is especially so when others possess knowledge and ideas that will allow you to improve upon your course of action.

- While a Starfleet officer is expected to succeed at all his duties and assignments, he must also have the strength of character to experience and recover from failure.

- Aboard a starship, an officer is often met by

traumatic situations that are sudden, unexpected, and short-lived; but even in the most perilous of conditions, you are expected to maintain your composure and assist others in maintaining theirs. The fact is, overcome by panic and despair, anyone can commit a mortal mistake.

- When met by mistakes or misfortune there is nothing to be gained by running away. Running away neither solves problems nor soothes feelings.

And last, but not least,

- We must recognize that in the most dire circumstances, an officer must retain a sense of hope— trusting in his own ability and in the competence of others to stand firm against what would otherwise be an overpowering tide of helplessness and gloom.

By way of concluding my thoughts on resilience, I assure you that as a Starfleet officer, your training and values will enable you to sustain even long periods of hardship while retaining some measure of hope—the mortality fail-safe of human will. Make it so.

Epilogue

Superintendent's note. *In his seven-plus years as captain of the* U.S.S. Enterprise-D, *Jean-Luc Picard led a starship whose myriad voyages and diverse missions afforded her crew a lifetime of remarkable experiences in but a short period. Both this starship and her crew will long be remembered for the path of understanding they propagated throughout the galaxy. Indeed, the crew of the Federation's flagship explored strange new worlds, discovered new life and new civilizations, and boldly went where no one had gone before.*

Admiral Andrea Brand
Superintendent, Starfleet Academy

Captain's personal journal: Stardate 48794.3.
En route to Earth.

My original intention for preparing this journal was to make a contribution to the leadership training of future cadets at Starfleet Academy. Notwithstanding, as I reflect upon them, the lessons contained in this record are worthy of periodic review throughout an officer's career, as they are root leadership qualities that apply to every level of command. While I have made every attempt to be concise yet thorough in this journal, I feel obligated to offer a final message of caution and perspective.

As a young ensign I believed that my performance as a junior officer would come under close examination. I also held the notion that as I progressed to more senior rank, I would be subjected to less scrutiny. However, I have come to understand this is not true. Although a junior officer's achievements can benefit others, his miscalculations can do only moderate harm. To this end, a junior officer should be recognized when he succeeds, critiqued when he errs, and forgiven for his honest mistakes. It follows that although a senior officer's achievements can benefit the common good, his miscalculations can result in widespread damage. To this end, a senior officer should be recognized for adding value to the lives of others, reprimanded when he errs, and expected to make but few honest mistakes.

Whatever his rank or position, an officer will always be subjected to scrutiny. However, just as it is wrong to praise an officer for the achievements of others, it is not right than an officer should have to account for another's shortcomings. However, I must caution you that you may indeed be unjustly scrutinized at some point in your career, just as my crew and I have been on occasion for the past seven years.

The first voyage of the *Starship Enterprise*-D was to Deneb IV, where Farpoint Station had been built by the Bandi, who inhabited that world. My mission was to negotiate a friendly agreement with the Bandi, to use their starbase, and at the same time to discover the mystery of Farpoint Station, which was how did the Bandi build such a magnificent starbase to Starfleet's precise specifications in just a short period of time?

En route to Deneb IV, we were to meet Q for the first time. Q is an omnipotent being who is part of an all-knowing super race known as "the Q," which exists in the Q Continuum—an extradimensional domain. After causing the *Enterprise* to come to a complete stop, Q appeared on the bridge and said to me, "Thou art notified that thy kind have infiltrated the galaxy too far already. Thou are directed to return to thy own solar system immediately."

Q went on to accuse humans of being a dangerous, savage, childlike race and too barbarous to expand. He said our race had slaughtered millions in arguments over how to divide the resources of our silly little world and that humans had earlier murdered each other in quarrels over tribal god images. Moreover, since those times there had been no indications that humans would ever change.

I admitted to Q that his allegations were once true of humanity; however, we had made rapid progress since then. I told him that he was one of those self-righteous life-forms, who was eager not to learn, but to prosecute and judge anything they didn't understand or couldn't tolerate.

Clearly the presence of this immensely powerful entity on my bridge was frightening, and I believed him to pose an immediate threat to our survival and acted on that premise. Placing Lieutenant Junior Grade Worf in command of the saucer section, I ordered him to evacuate all families and the majority of the ship's company to it. I transferred command of the *Enterprise* to the battle bridge and planned to engage the hostile force while allowing the saucer section to escape. The saucer separation was successful, and Mr. Worf was able to take his passengers out of harm's way. I then surrendered the battle bridge to Q, without terms or conditions.

Within moments, Lieutenant Commander Data, Lieutenant Commander Troi, Lieutenant Yar, and I found ourselves sitting in a courtroom set in the late twenty-first century—the postatomic horror period— and being heckled by all sorts of odd people dressed in clothing from that period. As the people in the gallery continuously mocked and laughed at us, the judge's bench came gliding toward us and stopped in the middle of the courtroom. Q was sitting at the bench, dressed in a judge's robe like those worn in the year 2079. Indeed, three of my staff and I were being put on trial to answer for multiple and grievous savageries of our species.

I informed Q that we would only answer to specific charges, whereupon I was handed a copy of the charges being brought against us. On reading these charges, I found none of them to be charges against us. Q then directed his armed bailiffs to ready their weapons. He then asked me how I pleaded to the charges and warned me that any answer other than "guilty" would result in Data, Troi, and Tasha's deaths.

My answer was "guilty," but provisionally so. While I could agree that humans had been savage in the past, we should not be tried for past savageries and should be judged on our own merits. Essentially, what happened was that Q agreed to allow us to continue to Farpoint Station. Q appointed himself as the prosecutor, judge, and jury who would determine the merits of whatever actions we took while there.

We arrived at Farpoint Station, where Commander Riker, Dr. Crusher and her son Wesley, and Lieutenant Junior Grade La Forge joined my crew. Mr. Worf soon arrived with the saucer, and the first major duty I gave to Commander Riker was to rejoin the saucer and the bridge. I must report that Will performed this duty very well indeed.

We later discovered that the Bandi hadn't built the space station. Instead, they had coerced an alien creature—a shapeshifting life-form—into assuming the form of the space station. Soon after this discovery, we witnessed the appearance of the alien creature's mate, who had come to rescue its partner. Although the alien destroyed the old Bandi city in order to free its mate, I chose not to interfere even though Q was goading me to do so. As a result of our actions at Farpoint Station, a disappointed Q judged us to have passed this initial trial, but vowed that he would be back to test humanity again.

Indeed, Q did visit us on several subsequent occasions. On each of his visits, Q placed us in grave danger and thereby tried humanity by how we responded to his tests. Our challenge was to continue to prove that humanity had progressed and was no longer a savage, dangerous race, and that we could be trusted beyond our own solar system. Q is ever a menace, an antagonist, an uninvited guest, and yet I believe that he somehow wants to help humanity progress by allowing us to understand our limitations as well as our potential. Q has caused us to experience many trials, and we have successfully passed them all. Even so, Q has needlessly kept us on trial for the past seven years and has recently informed me that the trial never ends. Nevertheless, while we were at Farpoint Station, Commander Riker asked me what we were going to do in light of the fact that Q was testing us twenty-four hours a day and could decree the summary judgment to destroy us at any time. I told my Number One, "We are going to do exactly what we'd do if the Q never existed. If we're going to be damned, let's be damned for what we really are."

You must recognize that while you may not be unjustly tried and judged by someone like Q, history will judge humanity, in part, by your actions: by how each of you applies your potential, by what you make of your possibilities, by what you do with your discoveries, by your respect for life, by how well you understand others and how well you help them understand you, and by how you react to the unknown. Indeed, the trial of humanity never ends.

Despite setbacks, I would like to believe that over the past eight years the crew of the *Enterprise* has made a difference in the lives of the people of the Federation and perhaps those of many other peoples as well. Making a difference is not without challenges, nor are its triumphs without tragedies. As such, we have been tested and met with great joy and deep sorrow.

Although we have unraveled many mysteries and made numerous discoveries, much of the galaxy remains to be explored. For this reason, though its mantle may pass to another spacecraft, I have every confidence that the *Enterprise*'s continuing mission will remain one through which others, who live in new generations, can make a difference in their own time. Make it so!

will judge humanity, in part, by your attitudes to how
each of you are, lies your potential, to what you make of
your possibilities, by what you do with your experiences,
by your respect for life, by how well you understand
others, and how well you help them understand you,
and by your journey to its ultimate end; indeed, the ethic
of humanity never ends.

Despite setbacks, I would like to believe that over the
past other years, the crew of the Enterprise has made a
difference in the lives of the people of the Federation
and perhaps those of many other peoples as well.
Making a difference is not without challenges, nor are
the triumphs without tragedies. As such, we have been
tested time and again with great joy and deep sorrow.

Although we have unraveled many mysteries and
made numerous discoveries, much of the galaxy remains to be explored. But this reason, though life
cannot truly pass us and they separated, I still very
confident that the Enterprise's extraordinary mission
will remain the through which others who live in new
generations can make a difference in their own time
and in the...

A Brief History of STAR TREK:

"The Original Series to The Next Generation"

Chartered in A.D. 2161, the United Federation of Planets is an alliance of some 150 planetary governments and colonies, which are aligned for purposes of mutual trade, shared exploratory expeditions, scientific research and development, cultural exchange, diplomatic relations, and joint defensive operations. Generally referred to as "the Federation," this interstellar alliance is occasionally threatened by enemies from without and conspirators within. Standing stalwart against all enemies and true to its purposes, the Federation remains a strong and powerful alliance over two hundred years after its formation.

The Federation is governed by a council of representatives from member governments and colonies. Its Council chambers are located in San Francisco on the planet Earth. The Council is presided over by a president, whose office is in Paris. This legislative body is guided in both principle and law by the Constitution of the United Federation of Planets, which insures the mutual benefit and protection of member planets and individual citizens.

In the same year this alliance was formed, the Council chartered Starfleet Command as the Federation's operating authority for interstellar scientific research and development, for exploratory expeditions, and as its defensive agency. Starfleet headquarters are located in San Francisco with other command facilities located in various starbases throughout Federation space. This Federation agency operates according to Starfleet General Orders and Regulations.

Starships are the mobil platforms from which Starfleet Command conducts its operations throughout Federation space. Starfleet spacecraft are designated by the initials U.S.S., which stand for "United Starship." Vessels of Federation registry, but not part of Starfleet, are designated by the initials S.S., which stand for "Starship." The *U.S.S. Enterprise* is the Federation's flagship, its continuing mission "to explore strange new worlds, to seek out new life and new civilizations, to boldly go where no one has gone before."

Communication between Starfleet Command and its starships is conducted by means of a subspace radio communications network, which often proves inadequate owing to the vastness of Federation space in the interstellar system. Starship captains, therefore, are granted considerable latitude in interpreting policy when outside radio contact.

Starfleet Academy is the primary training facility for Starfleet officers. This four-year institution was established in 2161 at the Presidio of San Francisco on Earth. Admission to the Academy is highly competitive, only the best and the brightest applicants gain entrance.

To grasp the essence of the transition from STAR TREK: THE ORIGINAL SERIES to STAR TREK: THE NEXT GENERA-

TION, one only needs to understand the evolution of the various starships named *Enterprise.*

The first starship *Enterprise* bore registry number NCC-1701. Built at the San Francisco Yards, this Constitution-class vessel measured 289 meters in overall length. NCC-1701 was launched in 2245 under the command of Captain Robert April. He was succeeded in command by Captain Christopher Pike in 2250. In 2263, Captain James T. Kirk was appointed commander of this spacecraft and commanded it during its historic mission of exploration that lasted from 2264 to 2269. Refitted several times during her many years of service, this Starship was assigned to training duty at Starfleet Academy in 2284. One year later, a crisis situation in the Mutara Sector once again brought this vessel back into strategic service under the command of Captain Kirk. Unable to prevail against the onslaught of his foe, Captain Kirk ordered the destruction of this ship to prevent her capture by the Klingons.

The second *Enterprise* was originally commissioned in 2286 as the *U.S.S. Yorktown.* Later that year, NCC-1701-A was redesignated *Enterprise* and assigned to the command of Captain Kirk in recognition of the heroic action taken by him and his crew to save Earth from the effects of an alien intruder. Designed for deep-space research and exploration, this Constitution-class spacecraft measured 305 meters in overall length and was rushed into full service in 2287—before her shakedown tests and systems installation were completed. The *Enterprise*-A's accelerated first mission was one of intervention in a hostage crisis at Nimbus III. In 2293, NCC-1701-A was once again placed under the command of Captain Kirk and—over Kirk's objections—sent to escort Klingon Chancellor Gorkon and his party to a peace conference on Earth. En route, Chancellor Gorkon was assassinated by Starfleet, Federation, and Klingon forces who wanted this peace effort to fail. The peace conference was postponed and its site removed to Camp Khitomer. This time, the peace talks were a success, but not before Captain Kirk, commanding the *Enterprise*-A, aided by Captain Sulu, commanding the *U.S.S. Excelsior,* prevented a second effort to thwart them. These historic talks became known as the Khitomer Peace Conference, which marked the rapprochement between the Federation and the Klingon Empire.

Built at Starfleet's Antares Shipyards, the third *Enterprise* was modeled on the failed original experimental *Excelsior;* which—after some modifications—later proved to be a spaceworthy and cost-efficient spacecraft design. NCC-1701-B measured 467 meters in length and was involved in mapping over 142 star systems. This *Enterprise* was also instrumental in exploration beyond the Gourami Sector and in establishing *first contact* with seventeen previously unknown civilizations.

The fourth starship *Enterprise* bore registry number NCC-1701-C. An Ambassador-class spacecraft measuring 525 meters in length, she was built at the Earth Station McKinley facility. According to the *normal* timeline for the *Next Generation* series, it is presumed that this spacecraft was destroyed and all hands lost during a battle with the Romulans in 2344 near Narendra III, a Klingon outpost, while under the command of Captain Rachel Garrett. There are no further indications of what took place in this battle as, to this day, neither traces of this Starship's destruction nor survivors of its crew have ever been discovered. However, during the battle with the Romulans, an explosion opened a temporal rift, and the *Enterprise*-C was sent twenty-two years forward in time. This event resulted in the formulation of an *alternate* timeline in which the Federation fought the Klingon Empire in a lengthy war. In 2366, the Federation was near defeat when the *Enterprise*-C emerged from the temporal rift and encountered the *Enterprise*-D. In order to return to the normal timeline and to avert the war with the Klingons, it was necessary for the *Enterprise*-C to return to her proper time in history. This corrective action accomplished, the time flow was returned to normal and history was restored accordingly. Therefore, the normal timeline for the series contains the history remembered by the people of the Federation.

Commanded by Captain Jean-Luc Picard, the *Enterprise,* NCC-1701-D, was built at the Utopia Planitia Fleet Yards located above Mars and launched in 2263. A Galaxy-class vessel, she measured 641 meters in length and had sufficient facilities to comfortably house up to 6,500 personnel. While the *Enterprise*-D's primary mission was one of exploration, this vessel was equipped with extensive scientific laboratories; her defensive shielding systems and heavy armament also made this spacecraft a formidable battleship. Without question, NCC-1701-D represented Starfleet's most sophisticated achievement in multimission ship system design to date.

STAR TREK: THE NEXT GENERATION begins with the launching of the *Enterprise*-D under the command of Captain Picard. And, Captain Picard's command of the *U.S.S. Enterprise*-D ends about seven and a half years later with her destruction on Veridian III in the movie STAR TREK GENERATIONS.

Cast of Characters

Alkar, Ves. (Played by Chip Lucia.) A Lumerian ambassador and Federation mediator.

April, Robert T. First captain of the *U.S.S. Enterprise,* NCC-1701, he commanded the *Enterprise* during her first five-year mission of deep-space exploration.

Batanides, Marta. (Played by J.C. Brandy.) Academy classmate of Jean-Luc Picard. After graduation from the Academy, Ensign Batanides was transferred to Starbase Earhart, along with Ensign Picard and Ensign Zweller, to await her first deep-space assignment.

Ben. (Played by Bruce Beatty.) Civilian waiter in the Ten-Forward lounge aboard the *Enterprise*-D.

Boothby. (Played by Ray Walston.) The groundskeeper at Starfleet Academy.

Bractor. (Played by Armin Shimerman.) Captain of the Ferengi attack vessel *Kreechta.*

Brand, Andrea. (Played by Jacqueline Brookes.) Superintendent of Starfleet Academy.

Cast of Characters

Crusher, Beverly. (Played by Gates McFadden.) Chief medical officer aboard the *U.S.S. Enterprise*-D, and mother of Wesley Crusher. Dr. Crusher holds the rank of commander. From 2365 to 2366, she served as chief of Starfleet Medical.

Crusher, Jack R. (Played by Doug Wert.) Starfleet officer killed while serving aboard the *U.S.S. Stargazer* under the command of Captain Jean-Luc Picard. Husband to Beverly Crusher and father of Wesley Crusher.

Crusher, Wesley. (Played by Wil Wheaton.) Son of Jack and Beverly Crusher. His father was killed in 2354, when Wesley was five years old. He went to live on the *U.S.S. Enterprise*-D when his mother became that ship's chief medical officer. Wesley remained on board during the one year she served as chief of Starfleet Medical. Given a field commission to the rank of ensign while aboard the *Enterprise,* Wesley later attended Starfleet Academy. After becoming disenchanted with his studies, Wesley resigned his commission in 2370 while a student at the Academy, choosing instead to live among the American Indians on Dorvan V.

Dal, Joret. (Played by Don Reilly.) Cardassian soldier and Federation operative.

Data. (Played by Brent Spiner.) Second officer aboard the *U.S.S. Enterprise*-D. Data is a humanoid android so sophisticated that he is regarded as a sentient life-form with full civil rights. He holds the rank of lieutenant commander in Starfleet.

Dathon. (Played by Paul Winfield.) Tamarian captain who likens himself to Darmok in an attempt to establish communication with Captain Jean-Luc Picard.

Devor. (Played by Tim Russ.) Member of the group of technicians-cum-terrorists who attempted to steal trilithium resin from the *Enterprise*-D while she was docked at the Remmler Array.

Franklin, Matt. Starfleet ensign serving aboard the *U.S.S. Jenolen* when she crashed into the Dyson Sphere. Although he survived the crash, he died while inside the Jenolen's transporter buffer awaiting rescue.

Galen, Richard. (Played by Norman Lloyd.) Possibly the greatest archaeologist of the twenty-fourth century and professor at Starfleet Academy during the period when Jean-Luc Picard was a cadet.

Garrett, Rachel. (Played by Tricia O'Neil.) Captain of the *U.S.S. Enterprise,* NCC-1701-C. Vanished along with the *Enterprise*-C and her crew in 2344 near Narendra III.

Genestra, Sabin. (Played by Bruce French.) A Betazoid who was aide to Starfleet Admiral Norah Satie.

Gorkon, Ambassador. (Played by David Warner.) Leader of the Klingon High Council, assassinated in 2293 by forces who sought to block his efforts for peace with the United Federation of Planets.

Guinan. (Played by Whoopie Goldberg.) A civilian bartender at the Ten-Forward lounge aboard the *U.S.S. Enterprise*-D. Guinan's people were nearly wiped out by the Borg in the late twenty-third century. Possessing an unusual sense that extends beyond normal linear space-time, she also has remarkable intuition.

Haden, Admiral. (Played by John Hancock.) Starfleet admiral who confirmed Cardassian reports that the *U.S.S. Phoenix* had attacked and destroyed a Cardassian science station in violation of the Federation-Cardassian peace treaty.

Hanson, J. P. (Played by George Murdock.) Starfleet admiral who led the Federation defense against the Borg attack at Wolf 359 in early 2367.

Cast of Characters

Henry, Thomas. (Played by Earl Billings.) Starfleet admiral in charge of security who visited the *Enterprise*-D at the request of Admiral Norah Satie, who erroneously suspected a conspiracy aboard the Federation's flagship.

Hutchinson, Calvin. (Played by David Spielberg.) Starfleet officer and commander of Arkaria Base.

Jaxa, Sito. (Played by Shannon Hill.) A Bajoran who attended Starfleet Academy and later served aboard the *Enterprise*-D. Ensign Sito was killed during an away mission to return Joret Dal, a Cardassian soldier and Federation operative, to Cardassian space.

J'Ddan. (Played by Henry Woronicz.) Klingon exobiologist who was assigned to the *Enterprise*-D as part of a Federation-Klingon science exchange program.

Jellico, Edward. (Played by Ronny Cox.) Starfleet officer who commanded the *U.S.S. Cairo* and who was given temporary command of the *Enterprise*-D in 2369.

Kelsey. (Played by Marie Marshall.) Leader of a technician-cum-terrorist group that attempted to steal trilithium resin from the *Enterprise*'s warp core while at the Remmler Array to undergo a baryon sweep.

Kirk, James T. (Played by William Shatner.) Captain of the *U.S.S. Enterprise,* NCC-1701 and NCC-1701-A. Commanded the *Enterprise* during her historic five-year mission of exploration in 2264–2269.

Kiros. (Played by Patricia Tallman.) Member of the group of technicians-cum-terrorists who attempted to steal trilithium resin from the *Enterprise*-D while she was docked at the Remmler Array.

Kolrami, Sirna. (Played by Roy Brocksmith.) Zakdorn master strategist who served as a tactical consultant to the *Enterprise*-D during a battle simulation.

La Forge, Geordi. (Played by LeVar Burton.) As a lieutenant junior grade, he was first assigned to be a flight controller aboard the *U.S.S. Enterprise*-D. In 2365, he was promoted to lieutenant and assigned as chief engineer. Mr. La Forge was later promoted to the rank of lieutenant commander. Blind since birth, he wears a Visual Instrument and Sensory Organ Replacement (VISOR), which is a slim device worn over his eyes like a pair of glasses. His VISOR permits him vision in visible light and across much of the electromagnetic spectrum, including infrared and radio waves.

Lavelle, Sam. (Played by Dan Gauthier.) Starfleet ensign who served aboard the *Enterprise*-D.

Lemec, Gul. (Played by John Durbin.) Captain of the Cardassian warship *Reklar*.

Locutus of Borg. (Played by Patrick Stewart.) Borg leader created by the assimilation of Jean-Luc Picard into the Borg consciousness in 2366.

Macet, Gul. (Played by Marc Alaimo.) Captain of the Cardassian warship *Trager*.

Madred, Gul. (Played by David Warner.) Cardassian captain who interrogated and tortured Captain Jean-Luc Picard at Celtris III in 2369.

Manheim, Jenice. (Played by Michelle Phillips.) Wife to scientist Dr. Paul Maxwell. Prior to her marriage, Jenice had been romantically involved with future Starfleet captain Jean-Luc Picard.

Maxwell, Benjamin. (Played by Bob Gunton.) Starfleet captain of the *U.S.S. Phoenix,* who destroyed a Cardassian science station in violation of the Federation-Cardassian peace treaty.

Mogh. Father to Worf and Kurn, and political rival to Ja'rod. Mogh and his wife were killed in the Khitomer massacre of

2346, after following Ja'rod to Khitomer because Mogh suspected him of disloyalty to the Klingon Empire.

Nechayev, Alynna. (Played by Natalia Nogulich.) Vice-admiral and Starfleet officer who was responsible for the handling of the Celtris III incident in 2369.

Neil. (Played by Tom Nibley.) Member of the group of technicians-cum-terrorists who attempted to steal trilithium resin from the *Enterprise*-D while she was docked at the Remmler Array.

O'Brien, Miles. (Played by Colm Meany.) A Starfleet engineer, he held the rank of ensign when first assigned to the *U.S.S. Enterprise*-D as the battle bridge conn officer. Commonly called "Chief" O'Brien, he later became chief of transporter-room operations on the *Enterprise*. In 2369, he was promoted and assigned as chief of operations on station *Deep Space Nine.*

Ogawa, Alyssa. (Played by Patti Yasutake.) Starfleet officer and nurse stationed aboard the *Enterprise*-D.

Orton, Mr. (Played by Glenn Morshower.) Station administrator of the Federation's Arkaria Base.

Picard, Jean-Luc. (Played by Patrick Stewart.) Captain of the *U.S.S. Enterprise*-D, which is the flagship of the United Federation of Planets. Captain Picard is a distinguished Starfleet officer who is also a noted figure in space exploration, science, and interstellar diplomacy.

Picard, Marie. (Played by Samantha Eggar.) Wife to Robert Picard, Jean-Luc Picard's sister-in-law, and mother of René Picard.

Picard, Maurice. (Played by Clive Church.) Vinticulturist from LaBarre, France. Husband to Yvette Gessard Picard, and father of Robert and Jean-Luc Picard.

Picard, René. (Played by David Tristen Birkin.) Son of Robert and Marie Picard, nephew of Jean-Luc Picard. René wanted to be like Jean-Luc and dreamed of one day that he would be leaving LeBarre for his own Starship.

Picard, Robert. (Played by Clive Church.) Son of Maurice and Yvette Gessard Picard, husband to Marie Picard, father of René Picard, and brother of Jean-Luc Picard. Robert followed in his father's footsteps and became a vinticulturist and took over operation of the Picard family vineyard.

Pike, Christopher. (Played by Jeffrey Hunter.) Early captain of the *U.S.S. Enterprise,* NCC-1701.

Powell, Lieutenant. Starfleet officer stationed aboard the *Enterprise*-D, who was romantically involved with Nurse Ogawa.

Pulaski, Katherine. (Played by Diana Muldaur.) A physician who showed remarkable empathy for her patients, she served as chief medical officer on the *U.S.S. Enterprise*-D during the year 2365. Dr. Pulaski held the rank of commander in Starfleet.

Q. (Played by John DeLancie.) An extradimensional entity possessing omnipotent powers, he also has a sense of child-like petulance and playfulness. Q has no compassion for the human race and loves to taunt and terrorize them as well as other species. Q both tormented and taught Captain Picard—at once both his nemesis and mentor—throughout Jean-Luc's command of the *Enterprise*-D.

Quinn, Gregory. (Played by Ward Costello.) Starfleet admiral who offered Captain Jean-Luc Picard a promotion to the rank of admiral and appointment as commandant of Starfleet Academy.

Riker, William T. (Played by Jonathan Frakes.) Executive officer and second-in-command of the *U.S.S. Enterprise*-D.

Cast of Characters

Holding the rank of commander in Starfleet, in his position he is also referred to as the ship's first officer. Often called "Number One" by Captain Picard, he has turned down command of several starships in order to remain on board the *Enterprise,* a ship he aspires to one day command.

Sarek. (Played by Mark Lenard.) Vulcan ambassador to the United Federation of Planets and father to Spock.

Satie, Norah. (Played by Jean Simmons.) Starfleet admiral who signed the order appointing Jean-Luc Picard as captain of the *U.S.S. Enterprise*-D. She was subsequently brought out of retirement and sent by Starfleet Command to assist Captain Picard with the investigation of suspected espionage and sabotage aboard the *Enterprise.*

Satler. (Played by Tim de Zarn.) Member of the group of technicians-cum-terrorists who attempted to steal trilithium resin from the *Enterprise*-D while she was docked at the Remmler Array.

Scott, Montgomery. (Played by James Doohan.) Also known as "Scotty," he was chief engineer aboard the first *Starship Enterprise,* which was commanded by Captain James T. Kirk.

Shelby, Lieutenant Commander. (Played by Elizabeth Dennehy.) Officer who was placed in charge of Starfleet's planning for defense against the Borg in early 2366.

Solok, DaiMon. (Played by Lou Wagner.) Ferengi smuggler who sometimes ran cargo to Celtris III.

Sulu, Hikaru. (Played by George Takei.) Helm officer aboard the first *Enterprise* under the command of Captain Kirk. He was later to captain the *U.S.S. Excelsior.*

Tarses, Simon. (Played by Spencer Garrett.) Crewman first class and medical technician aboard the *Enterprise*-D, he was falsely accused by Admiral Satie of being a Romulan spy.

Taurik, Ensign. (Played by Alexander Enberg.) A Vulcan who attended Starfleet Academy and served as an engineer under the command of Lieutenant Commander Geordi La Forge aboard the *Enterprise*-D.

Tore, Nellen. (Played by Ann Shea.) A native of Delb II and assistant to Admiral Norah Satie.

Troi, Deanna. (Played by Marina Sirtis.) Ship's counselor on board the *U.S.S. Enterprise*-D, Counselor Troi held the rank of lieutenant commander when first assigned to that starship. She was later promoted to the rank of commander. She is the daughter of Ian Andrew and Lwaxana Troi. Her father being human and her mother being Betazoid, Counselor Troi has the ability to sense powerful emotions in most life-forms.

Worf. (Played by Michael Dorn.) Graduating from the Academy in 2361, Worf became the first Klingon to serve Starfleet. Holding the rank of lieutenant junior grade when first assigned to the *U.S.S. Enterprise*-D as flight control officer, he was later promoted to lieutenant and was assigned as the *Enterprise*'s chief of security.

Yar, Natasha. (Played by Denise Crosby.) Lieutenant and chief of security aboard the *U.S.S. Enterprise*-D during 2364. She was killed later that year while participating in a rescue mission on planet Vagra II.

Zweller, Cortin. (Played by Ned Vaughn.) Academy classmate of Jean-Luc Picard. After graduation from the Academy, Ensign Zweller was transferred to Starbase Earhart, along with Ensign Picard and Ensign Batanides, to await his first deep-space assignment.

Key Terms

(As drawn from *The Star Trek Encyclopedia* by Michael Okuda, Denise Okuda, and Debbie Mirek)

antimatter. Matter whose electrical charge properties are opposite of "normal" matter. When a particle of antimatter is brought into contact with an equivalent particle of normal matter, both particles are annihilated, and a large amount of energy is released.

away team. Starfleet term for a specialized squad of personnel sent on a mission away from the ship, usually on a planet's surface.

communicator. A personal communications device contained within the insignia badge worn by Starfleet personnel. Communicators also emit a signal that can be used to locate the person wearing the badge. This feature provides a Starship's transporter system the means for determining exact coordinates, which are necessary for transporting personnel from one location to another.

conn. Abbreviation for flight controller.

Key Terms

"Darmok and Jalad at Tenagra." A Tamarian phrase that referred to a mythological hunter on planet Shantil III and his companion Jalad, who met and shared a danger at the mythical island of Tanagra. See: Dathon listed in Cast of Characters.

deflectors. Energy field used to protect starships and other vessels from harm resulting from natural hazards or enemy attack.

dom-jot. Billiards-like game with an irregularly shaped table.

holodeck. Also known as a Holographic Environment Simulator, the holodeck permits the simulation of virtually any environment or person with a degree of fidelity virtually indistinguishable from reality.

impulse drive. Spacecraft propulsion system using conventional impulse reactions to generate thrust. Aboard most Federation starships, impulse drive is powered by one or more fusion reactors that employ deuterium fuel to yield helium plasma and a lot of power. A ship under impulse drive is limited to slower-than-light speeds. Normally, full impulse is about half the speed of light.

Number One. A common name given by Starship captains to their second-in-command.

padd. Acronym for personal access display device. Small handheld information unit used by Starfleet personnel aboard Federation starships.

phaser. Acronym for PHASed Energy Rectification, a directed energy weapon used by Starfleet and others. Phaser energy can be adjusted to a variety of settings including stun, heat, and disruption. Phaser weapons range from handheld sidearms, to rifles, and to large ship-mounted weapons.

Key Terms

photon torpedo. Tactical weapon used by Federation starships. Photon torpedoes are self-propelled missiles containing a small quantity of matter and antimatter bound together in a magnetic bottle.

Prime Directive. Also known as Starfleet General Order #1, the Prime Directive mandates that Starfleet personnel and spacecraft are prohibited from interfering in the normal development of any society, and that any Starfleet vessel or crew member is expendable to prevent violation of this rule.

sensors. Generic term for a wide range of scientific, medical, and engineering instruments used aboard Federation starships and in other applications.

Seventh Guarantee. One of the fundamental civil liberties protected by the Constitution of the United Federation of Planets. It protects citizens against self-incrimination.

shields. Energy field used to protect Starships and other vessels form harm resulting from natural hazards or enemy attack. The transporter cannot function when shields are active.

stardate. Timekeeping system used to provide a standard galactic temporal reference, compensating for relativistic time dilation, warp-speed displacement, and other peculiarities of interstellar space travel.

strategema. Challenging holographic game of strategy and wills. Played by two contestants, the game involves manipulating circular icons on a three-dimensional grid to gain control of one's opponent's territory while defending your own.

tractor beam. A focused linear graviton force beam used to physically manipulate objects across short distances.

transporter. Matter-energy conversion device used to provide a convenient means of transportation. The transporter briefly converts an object or person into energy, beams that energy to another location, then reassembles the subject into its original form.

tricorder. Multipurpose scientific and technical instrument. This handheld device incorporates sensors, computers, and recorders in a convenient, portable form.

turbolift. Starfleet term for a high-speed elevator system used aboard Federation starships for intraship personnel transport.

viewer. Visual display screens used aboard Federation starships. Viewers can be small desktop devices intended for personal use, or can be large wall-mounted units. Also called viewscreen and screen.

VISOR. A slim bioelectrical device worn over the face like a pair of glasses, VISOR is the acronym for Visual Instrument and Sensory Organ Replacement. One of these devices was worn by Geordi La Forge, who was born blind. The VISOR permits vision in visible light as well as across much of the electromagnetic spectrum including infrared and radio waves. While providing Geordi with better-than-normal sight, wearing this device also caused him continuous pain.

warp drive. Primary propulsion system used by most faster-than-light interstellar spacecraft. Federation starships employ the controlled annihilation of matter and antimatter regulated by dilithium crystals to power their warp drive.

warp factor. Unit of measure used to measure faster-than-light velocities. Warp factor one is c, the speed of light. By the twenty-fourth century, a new warp factor scale was in use that employed an asymptotic curve, placing warp ten as an infinite value.

References

Books

Johnson, Shane. *Star Trek: The Worlds of the Federation.* New York: Pocket Books, 1989.

Nemecek, Larry. *The Star Trek: The Next Generation Companion.* New York: Pocket Books, 1992.

Okrand, Marc. *The Klingon Dictionary.* New York: Pocket Books, 1992.

Okuda, Michael, and Denise Okuda and Debbie Mirek. *The Star Trek Encyclopedia: A Reference Guide to the Future.* New York: Pocket Books, 1994.

Okuda, Michael, and Denise Okuda. *Star Trek Chronology: The History of the Future.* New York: Pocket Books, 1993.

Sternbach, Rick, and Michael Okuda. *Star Trek: The Next Generation Technical Manual.* New York: Pocket Books, 1991.

References

Principal Episodes

Chain of Command, Part 1. Episode number: 236. Teleplay by Ronald D. Moore. Story by Frank Abatemarco. Directed by Robert Scheerer.

Chain of Command, Part 2. Episode number: 237. Written by Frank Abateman. Directed by Les Landau.

Coming of Age. Episode number: 119. Written by Sandy Fries. Directed by Michael Vejar.

Darmok. Episode number: 202. Teleplay by Joe Monosky. Story by Philip Lazebnik and Joe Menosky. Directed by Winrich Kolbe.

Encounter at Farpoint, Part 1. Episode number: 101. Written by D. C. Fontana and Gene Roddenberry. Directed by Corey Allen.

Encounter at Farpoint, Part 2. Episode number: 102. Written by D. C. Fontana and Gene Roddenberry. Directed by Corey Allen.

Lower Decks. Episode number: 267. Teleplay by René Echevarria. Story by Ronald Wilkerson and Jean Louise Matthias. Directed by Gabrielle Beaumont.

Peak Performance. Episode number: 147. Written by David Kemper. Directed by Robert Scheerer.

Relics. Episode number: 230. Written by Ronald D. Moore. Directed by Alexander Singer.

Starship Mine. Episode number: 244. Written by Morgan Gendel. Directed by Cliff Bole.

Tapestry. Episode number: 241. Written by Ronald D. Moore. Directed by Les Landau.

The Best of Both Worlds, Part 1. Episode number: 174. Written by Michael Piller. Directed by Cliff Bole.

References

The Best of Both Worlds, Part 2. Episode number: 175. Written by Michael Piller. Directed by Cliff Bole.

The Drumhead. Episode number: 195. Written by Jeri Taylor. Directed by Jonathan Frakes.

The First Duty. Episode number: 219. Written by Ronald D. Moore and Naren Shankar. Directed by Paul Lynch.

The Wounded. Episode number: 186. Teleplay by Jeri Taylor. Story by Stuart Charno, Sara Charno, and Cy Chermak. Directed by Chip Chalmers.

Acknowledgments

This book would not have been possible without the genius and imagination of Gene Roddenberry, who created STAR TREK, Robert H. Justman, Rick Berman, Michael Piller, Jeri Taylor, and the dedication and talent of all others who have made and continue to make STAR TREK a worldwide entertainment phenomenon. We would like to acknowledge the excellent creative work of those people who wrote the episodes retold in this work. They include: Frank Abatemarco, Sara Charno, Stuart Charno, Cy Chermak, René Echevarria, D. C. Fontana, Sandy Fries, Morgan Gendel, David Kemper, Philip Lazebnik, Jean Louise Matthias, Joe Menosky, Ronald D. Moore, Michael Piller, Gene Roddenberry, Naren Shankar, Jeri Taylor, and Ronald Wilkerson. We would also like to acknowledge the authors who wrote the reference books from which we were able to gain vital facts and information. These authors include: Shane Johnson, Debbie Mirek, Larry Nemecek, Marc Okrand, Denise Okuda, Michael Okuda, and Rick Sternbach. Besides the

Acknowledgments

people who have brought us STAR TREK, we owe a debt of gratitude to the millions of STAR TREK enthusiasts—Trekkers—who have made STAR TREK an icon of twentieth-century popular culture.

As this book is based on the character he played, it is fitting to acknowledge Patrick Stewart for his grand performances as Captain Jean-Luc Picard, a fictional character who commands respect around the world. It is also appropriate to recognize the other actors who played the major characters that helped make STAR TREK: THE NEXT GENERATION so familiar to people everywhere. They are: Jonathan Frakes, Gates McFadden, Brent Spiner, LeVar Burton, Marina Sirtis, Michael Dorn, Wil Wheaton, Denise Crosby, Diana Muldaur, Whoopi Goldberg, John DeLancie, Colm Meaney, and Majel Barrett Roddenberry.

It is also appropriate to acknowledge the assistance of those persons who have been directly involved with the production of this work. To that end, we thank Richard Pine for placing this book with Pocket Books. Special thanks go to Arthur Pine, Lori Andiman, and Sara Piel of Arthur Pine Associates, who have given us their support and encouragement throughout this project. We are especially grateful to Kevin Ryan at Pocket Books for his excellent editing of this book and for providing direction and guidance during its preparation. Jack Romanos, president of Simon & Schuster Consumer Group, is acknowledged for his enthusiastic support and special interest in this project.

We would also like to thank Justin Roberts for assisting with the general structure and approach for this book. Many thanks to Jeremy Roberts for helping identify the episodes used to illustrate each of the book's chapters, for assisting with the preparation of the epilogue, and for proofreading drafts of the manuscript. Our thanks to Jaime Roberts for proofreading and helping with many administrative details related to this book's preparation. A special word of appreci-

Acknowledgments

ation to Cheryl Roberts for helping put this entire project together and for her efforts that clarified several important points and cleaned up the syntax in the manuscript. We would also like to acknowledge Susan Ross for watching episodes of STAR TREK: THE NEXT GENERATION to help identify stock phrases used by Captain Picard. We extend our appreciation to Major General Robert Coffey, Brigadier General John Le Moyne, Command Sergeant Major Wayne Sills, and other leaders of the U.S. Army's 2nd Armored Division for helping fine-tune several of the more subtle leadership precepts in this book during Wess's visit to the National Training Center at Fort Irwin, California. We are indebted to Randy Staples, Michael Sullivan, and Doug Hansen for reading and commenting on the manuscript; their suggestions were timely and useful. Also, thanks to Chett Paulsen for providing several suggestions that helped improve this book.

Bill would also like to take this opportunity to thank other members of his family for their support in his life and career. They include: his parents, Lee and Al; his sister Lin; his brother Raym; and his son, Rusty.